Championship
DINGHY
SAILING

—

CHRISTOPHER CASWELL

DAVID ULLMAN

D0127035

W · W · NORTON & COMPANY · INC · NEW YORK

Photographs are by Christopher Caswell.

Designer: Marjorie J. Flock

Library of Congress Cataloging in Publication Data
Caswell, Christopher.
    Championship dinghy sailing.
    Includes index.
    1. Sailing.   2. Sailboat racing.   I. Ullman,
David, joint author.   II. Title.
GV811.6.037   797.1'4   77-5536
ISBN 0-393-03205-1

Championship
DINGHY
SAILING

Contents

Foreword

FAST AND FURIOUS is perhaps an understatement for the level of competition in dinghy classes. Nowhere in the world of sailboat racing can be found such a depth of talent and such a continuous pitch of activity as in the centerboard classes. This constant intensity, combined with the ability to buy a fully equipped and competitive boat for a reasonable price, is what lures thousands and thousands of sailors to the myriad fleets of these boats. This book is dedicated to these classes and these sailors.

Too many books on sailing try to cover the entire field of racing from tiny prams to mighty ocean racers, and they end up doing nothing well. Racing theory alone is fine, if you do all your sailing in a wind tunnel. But if, as Teddy Roosevelt commented, you're the one in the arena with sweat on your brow, you'd better have some practical advice.

So this book is full of the nitty-gritty. It is one man's approach to championship dinghy racing. There are no essays on racing rules or dissertations on weather, because good books exist on those subjects. What we offer are years of racing distilled into practical advice. They are the thoughts of one highly successful sailor, Dave Ullman, combined with my own modest racing successes and journalistic abilities.

All the first-person thoughts in this book (after this foreword) are Dave's, and he's uniquely qualified to discuss two-man centerboarders. Born into a sailing family, Dave started racing at an early age and had won four national championships by his eighteenth birthday. He went on to take a third at the Snipe nationals in his first try and, in the following years, came back with two fourths, a third, two seconds, and finally the national title in 1973. In the same year, he was sixth in the Snipe worlds' championship and won the Pan American Trials in the following year.

Jumping into the 470 class in 1972, he promptly won both the national and North American championships. He was first at CORK in '73, swept the nationals in '74, and placed fourth in the world's. The 1975 nationals went to Dave again, along with the Pre-Olympic Trials.

Not content to sail just Snipes and 470s, he also picked up three Sabot national championships, a nationals in the Coronado 15, and four nationals (out of five tries) in Lido 14s during these same years. In one year, he held national titles in 470, Lido 14, Sabot, and Coronado 15.

My own sailing credentials are pale in this reflected light, but my trophy shelves bear hardware in classes ranging from Lido 14s to Flying Dutchmen. My chief contribution to this book was to pry loose, with tape recorder and endless questions, the thinking that has led Dave Ullman to the position of one of the fastest men afloat.

At one yacht club where Dave was lecturing, a man turned to his wife and whispered, "You know, if I could just remember five percent of what he says, we'd finish in the top five in every race!"

That, then, is the message . . .

Christopher Caswell

PRE-RACE: THE BOAT

Chapter 1

THE BEST WAY to start a book like this is to assume that the reader is in the process of buying a boat. It's the best way because it permits some basic recommendations that too many people tend to overlook.

I think you can break sailboat racing down into two basic types: Olympic and casual. Olympic racing is just what it sounds like—racing an Olympic class boat with the goal of reaching and possibly winning the Olympic Games. Olympic racing can really include a lot of other types of serious racing, but the sailors who truly fit this category can never be confused with casual racers. A sailor can be at the Olympic level in a non-Olympic class, but he always seems to wind up taking a shot at the Olympic Games sooner or later.

On the other hand, casual racing includes all other types of dinghy racing. Casual racing is perhaps a misnomer, because there is rarely anything casual about the heat of the competition. The "casual" applies more to the long term commitment to that particular class. Where an Olympic racer will think nothing of buying hundreds of dollars worth of new sails, masts, or even boats, the casual racer usually works within a much more modest budget. He doesn't automatically figure in thousands of miles of traveling to regattas in his yearly budget, nor does he block out weeks at a time when he does nothing but sail in one series after another, as the Olympic sailor may do. If a sailor decides to opt for Olympic-level competition, he should plan to travel.

Money is another major criterion that should affect the new boat decision. I assume that everyone reading this book wants to win sailboat races, but if he doesn't have a certain realistic approach to costs, then he'll never do it. In Olympic-level racing, you just can't do well with one suit of sails and one mast. You can't wait for your equipment to wear out before you buy something new. You have to buy whatever is fastest at that time and be fully prepared to discard it in two months for something faster. Even the basic hull is expendable; you have to be prepared to pick up the tab for a faster hull. The investment of money is a basic premise of this type of racing.

For those of you interested in Olympic racing, what I've just said sounds terribly negative. It isn't. I'm just assuming that you want to win—not just the Sunday club races but the bigger events like fleet championships, districts, even take a stab at the nationals. Just be prepared for the commitment that Olympic racing demands. I'll get to my thoughts on the Olympics themselves in a moment.

If Olympic racing (or its rigors) doesn't appeal to you, then go for casual racing. People can race competitively with two-year-old sails and no traveling fund. In a lot of casual classes, the outright boatspeed is lower so that your basic sailing ability counts for more than fancy equipment. The whole choice is purely a question of your own attitude. And let me confess that I enjoy racing a Lido-14 with my wife as much as I enjoy sailing in the 470 World Championship.

Too many people choose Olympic racing when they should have chosen the more casual style. They find out later that they connected Olympic racing with hot racing, which is not true. Sure, the Olympic boats have keen competition, but so do a myriad of local classes. Some people in the 470 class are bitter about the price of the boat and the continual sail changing and so forth; they're in the wrong class. They should be in a class that has good racing at lower pressure.

Too many people are also lured by the "power and glory" or the Olympic atmosphere, when they should really be enjoying good fleet racing every weekend in something like a Lido-14 or a Snipe.

So make your cut to either the rich-man or the poor-man class, and then look around your own area to see what is avilable. It doesn't make any sense at all to choose a class where the nearest large fleet is 500 miles away unless you're some kind of driving fetishist. Every area has some good racing class—it may be a local one-design like the Lido, or it may be a regional outpost of an international class like the Snipe. But believe me, it's always more fun to sail against thirty other skippers than to sail against just five. By the same token, too many people pick a class where they know they can win. Being a big frog in a little pond and winning all the time doesn't improve you at all, and it soon gets boring.

Another strong point for most of the casual classes is that they're more than happy to help new people along. Some schedule clinics where techniques and tactics are discussed by the local hotshots, and others stage races where a winning skipper will crew for you. In the Olympic classes, you'll find you're on your own. With the exception of the class officers, the 470 class doesn't help anybody, but that's a symptom of the high level of competition. People are more private about their boats and styles because more is at stake.

I think Olympic fever is the worst thing in yachting. It takes all the fun out of racing. People get too serious about it. And I don't know why they're so much more serious about the Olympics than they would be over their own world championship. In every class I know, the world's are far tougher to win than the Olympics. Take the 470 class as an example. In a country like France, which has a lot of 470 racing, there are nine men who are capable of winning the world championship. Only one can sail in the Olympics, but all nine sail in the world's. That just has to give the fleet a depth of talent that is amazing.

But although I don't know what it is about the Olympics that has such an attraction, I'm hooked just as certainly as the others. Who am I to criticize?

Getting back to your choice of boats, once you've made your

basic choice and then studied the various boats that have good racing in your area, take a look at yourself. I'm five feet, five inches tall and I weigh about 110 pounds, so I try to sail small boats where my size is an asset rather than a detriment. On a competitive level, my size should help me win, not hinder me, but I see people fooling themselves all the time.

For example, a 470 does best with a small skipper and a big crew; their total combined weight should be about 270 to 275 pounds. The skipper shouldn't weigh over 140 pounds, but a lot of people think they can sail a 470 at a weight of 170 pounds. There's just no way they'll ever be competitive, because their size will hold them back.

Take a look at your crew, too. If you plan to sail man-woman, give some thought to a boat that has an easily handled jib and no spinnaker. If you plan to sail two-man, then look toward a boat with trapeze and spinnaker where you can flex your collective muscles.

There are still more factors to consider. In the 470, agility is a prime factor—so much so that thirty years of age seems to be the limit. Older or bigger (or slower) sailors should consider a Flying Dutchman or a Star for Olympic-level racing. The reverse seems to be true in a non-trapezing boat. I think the skipper, ideally, should be the larger and heavier of the two. The larger person is able to work the boat more effectively off the wind, especially when you have to synchronize rocking movements with sheeting action. A crew can never get it quite right. It doesn't seem to make much difference going to weather, except that the big skipper can hike a bit more and have a better view of the sails and waves.

I have trouble there (because of my size) which is why I've turned towards trapeze boats where my weight is an advantage. In fact, I even considered sailing a Flying Dutchman, simply because I could have a really huge crew.

So consider your commitment to the sport, your own area, and the size of you (and crew) before you pick your boat.

DECK LAYOUT

Chapter **2**

JUST AS in choosing a class, too many sailors jump into a new boat and try to make it an ultra racing machine with lots of shiny blocks and tricky adjustments. I think that's foolish. I don't even buy a bare hull and rig it myself usually. I just take what is given with the boat and, if necessary, rearrange it a bit.

A person approaching a new class should buy the hottest standard boat available at that time. In a lot of classes, like the Lido-14 and Coronado-15, there is only one builder, so the choice is irrelevant. In multi-builder classes, get the fastest boat. Sail it for at least six months before you even touch any of the fittings. Then decide what you want to change. You'll usually be surprised to find that many of the fittings or arrangements that you originally disliked will have become acceptable to you.

It's a lot easier to buy a good standard boat and rearrange the gear than it is to start from scratch. Most people don't really know what they want; they just think they know. Sail the boat and then make your changes. If you find you have radically different ideas that require a major upheaval, you should probably then consider buying a bare hull and rigging it.

People get too involved in hardware. It has to do a job—nothing more and nothing less. If what is on the standard boat does the job functionally, then it doesn't have to be changed to a new roller-double-swivel-whatzit. Don't worry about whether it's the very newest or the blackest or the shiniest. This isn't a fashion show. Your equipment has to do the job efficiently. It's too easy to look at another boat and see that it has a lever vang and you assume that you have to have one too. If it doesn't make the boat go through the water any faster, then don't worry about it. At the same time, there are some things you should be concerned with when rigging your boat.

Most small, high-performance boats are, or should be, using a continuous barber hauler system like the 505 (completely movable) or a standard fixed position jib lead that is well inboard along with a barber hauler that can pull the lead outboard to the rail. I find in some classes, like the Snipe, that going to weather we are no longer adjusting the jib lead. It stays all the way inboard, and we use the barber hauler strictly for the reaches. In fact, we've removed the barber hauler from my 470 because we weren't using it at all. But that decision is a function of the jib you have. Some jibs with a tight leach and aft draft demand a barber hauler when going to weather in a breeze. Open leached jibs don't need the wide sheeting base. On the jibs that I make we don't recommend barber hauling at all. The only time you need it is close reaching without a spinnaker, which we've experienced in only one race in three years of hard sailing. The course has to be set very poorly or the wind has to shift immensely; in both cases the race should be called anyway. So look at your jib and decide whether you really need a barber hauler at all. And if you do need it, use it!

On the Snipe, most people are going to a single jib track about sixteen inches from the center line, which seems pretty tight but it's very effective. That's about the same for the 470, or about six degrees off center. When the wind comes up, we just sheet a little looser so the sails aren't strapped and the slot opens slightly. The opposite school of thought applies to jibs with a flat entry and fairly tight leeches; with that type of sail you *have* to open the slot.

Most classes seem to be going to a leeward cleating of the jib sheet. There was a time when the sheet was led to the weather side, but I think that's a lot more awkward. The cleat should be on the leeward deck or attached to the block so that when the crew pulls the jib in, it automatically cleats. In the 470 and 505, it has to be a lot more exotic because you have to move fore and aft as well as be able to cleat and uncleat from the trapeze. We're using a combination of gear that is a bit complicated but it does the job . . . three different fittings welded together. Some people worry about losing the "feel" of the sheet when it runs through several blocks, but I think the jib should be trimmed visually and the feel isn't too important.

On our 470, the spinnaker sheet leads through the aft rail to a ratchet block on the transom and then forward to a turning block. (See Figure 1.) We don't have any cleats for it. The weather sheet—really the afterguy—goes to a reaching hook by the shroud and then to a cleat right behind the hook (see Figure 2). So you're really only playing the sheet and I don't have any conflict with lines leading around my legs except when I'm going dead downwind and both sheets are being played. By the way, the reaching hook cleat is the only place we use a clam cleat on the boat. We use a lot of the little Fico stainless steel cam cleats, though.

On the Snipe, we have a floating

Figure 1 ■ (*Above*)
Figure 2 ■ (*Below*)

luff jib where the tack is not attached to the luff wire; it has its own down-haul. The wire is attached to the boat (see Figure 3) at more tension than the headstay, and the jib is free to float up or down. I think it's the best system there is . . . if the class allows it. You get the best control over the jib shape as well as control over the mast rake. The only possible improvement would be to put the jib over the headstay it-self, which would eliminate the wind-age of the headstay.

On the Snipe, the halyards run in-ternally through the spar, so we don't have any problem with the lengths changing as the mast is bent. But on the Coronado 15, where the halyards are external, the halyard tension has to be readjusted as the spar bends. On the 470, it's different again because the rig is set up with a lot of tension (200-plus pounds) whereas the Snipe and C-15 have loose rigs. So the 470 jib luff tension is established by jib halyard tension. The halyard goes to a magic box (a multi-purchase block and tackle; see Figure 4) and we change the setting three or four times a race as the wind changes. That controls the mast rake also, since our headstay is really only there to comply with the

Figure 3 ▪

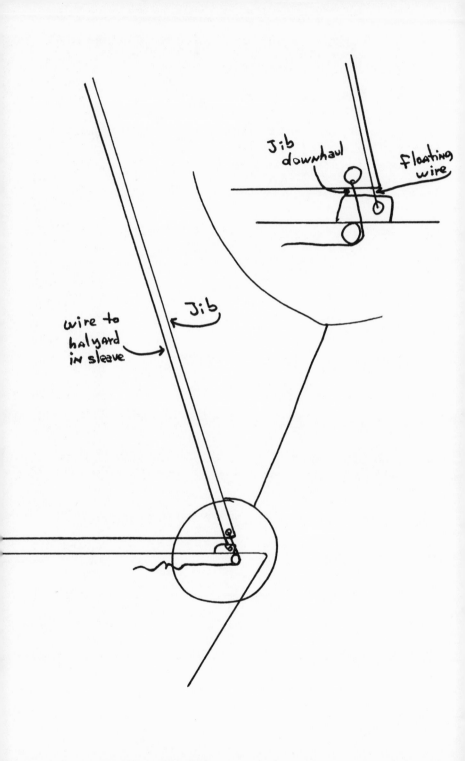

Jib
downhaul

floating
wire

wire to
halyard
in sleeve

Jib

Figure 4 ∎

rule. Our mast would fall over the side before the headstay went tight. By the way, having a loose headstay allows it to lie on the sail and create less wind drag than if it were creating turbulence right in front of the luff.

Mast partners are really important. They should be as stiff as possible and I wouldn't even recommend trying to save weight in them. They should be very tight sideways, even with loose rigs. If your class rules allow, you should be able to induce bend in either forward or aft directions. In the 470, you're only allowed to restrict bend in front of the mast. So it's important to "pre-bend" the mast in light airs to get the luff curve (the draft put into the luff by the sailmaker) out of the mainsail. In the 470, the mast restrictor also helps control the mast movement for more power on reaches. In the past, we've limited the mast bend in the 470 by wooden blocks (Figure 4-A) but the class now allows a wire around the front of the spar to a halyard ball system (see Figure 5) which gives you a better purchase. The

Figure 4–A ■ (*On facing page*) *The least effective method of mast adjustment are the wooden blocks in front of this 470 mast. Hard to adjust, they make fine tuning impossible.*

Figure 5 ■

block system is really ineffective. In the Snipe, we use a 24 to 1 lever that is bolted to the spar so the mast can be pushed or pulled in either direction, which is the ideal system.

Depending on your class's rules, do as much as you can to control the mast at the deck level; it's well worth it. Use a full push-pull lever if you can, or use an effective restricting system that can *easily* be adjusted.

Mainsheet rigs: It seems like most boats are changing to a center-traveler mainsheet rig now, but it's not that good. I think a stern traveler is best. You have much better boom control, you have easier sheeting loads, you reduce bending forces, and you can have a smaller boom. But the stern traveler provides a problem for the tiller. In the 470, you're permitted to use a stern traveler, and a few boats have them, but you have to take the center traveler out and that really weakens the boat. The structure of the 470 was designed to include that cross brace amidships, and the boat flexes without it. You gain a little in sail control with the stern traveler in this case, but you lose a lot more with the flexing.

On the Snipe, we put a block on a line with restricting lines to control its travel . . . which makes for a lot of gear on the stern. It gives good control, but you end up with double-sided controls and a great deal of line in the cockpit.

In the 470, the traveler has to be straight, by class rule. Some 505s have gone to a downward curve in the middle of the traveler, and I frankly don't understand that. In fact, I've seen some 505s with an up curve in the middle and that *really* doesn't make sense. The only possible reason I can see is that the higher middle forces you to sheet harder as the traveler and boom are eased, but you're stuck if you don't want that. The ideal traveler

Figure 6 ■ *A homemade lever boom vang on a 470. The aluminum arm increases the force applied to the boom immensely, and care must be taken not to bend the boom.*

system would be a level track curved in an even radius from the mast, so that the loads are constant as you ease the boom out.

The 505s, because of the inefficient mainsheet rig, have also gone to giant boom vangs for leech tension, which makes less sense. That really doesn't give you any control over the tension of the leech, because you have to adjust two things (Boom vang and sheet) just to control the main. I'd rather never adjust the vang and just use the traveler. A further 505 problem is that they have to use really heavy booms because the bend forces from the vang are so extreme. In the 470s, we don't have stiff enough booms yet. One 470 skipper who uses a lot of vang tension broke six booms in one season alone.

A lot of 470 sailors seem to be easing their traveler to leeward in too little wind. We keep our traveler to weather of centerline up to about 15 knots of wind. I think the traveler is even more important than the mainsheet. Some sailors use a mainsheet system that cleats on each side of the boat, which forces them to carry the sheet across the boat as they tack. With that method, it's a problem to get everything done: tack, carry the sheet across, adjust the traveler . . . all in less time than it takes to read this. I use a central jamb cleat on a swivel, so I only have to move the traveler as I tack.

On our 470, we have a continuous traveler line because about half the time I forget to uncleat one side as I tack. With the continuous line, I can flip it loose from the leeward cleat easily.

We pull the traveler to weather of the centerline about 10 inches, but we can pull it all the way to the end if we need to. That only gives you an extra couple of feet of line in the boat, and it's worth it when you need it.

In the Coronado-15, which has a very high boom, we sail with the traveler all the way to weather *all* the time. Basically what you want is to get the boom on centerline and the top batten parallel with the boom. On the C-15, it looks like you'll be over-trimmed with the traveler all the way to weather, but the boom is so high that the sheeting angle is the same as we use on the

470. The difference is that there's just a lot more mainsheet between the boom and the deck. So set your traveler wherever necessary to get the boom to centerline.

Spinnaker Launchers: Any class that can have a tube-type launcher should have one. In the 470, we are only allowed bags for spinnaker storage but, regardless of the method used, the spinnaker should set and douse easily, preferably without too much struggle from the crew.

Spinnaker Halyard: We have a 1 to 2 system (see Figure 7) so that for every foot of halyard I pull, it actually hoists two feet. Some people have even gone to a 1 to 3 or 4 system, but 1 to 2 is

Figure 7 ■ *Spinnaker halyard.*

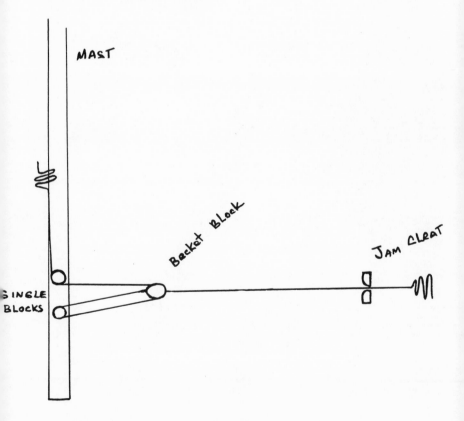

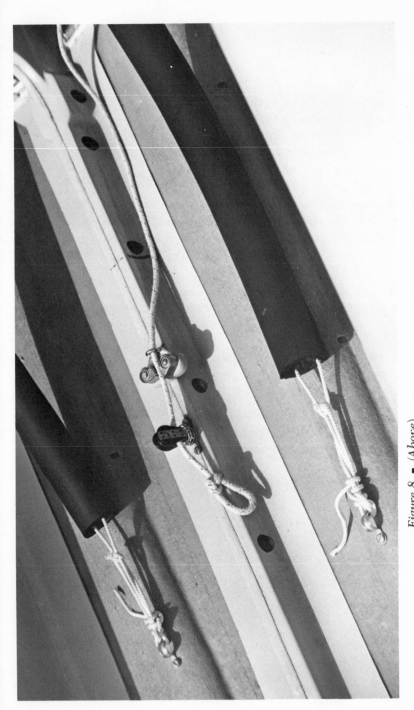

Figure 8 ■ (Above)
Figure 9 ■ (Below) *One way of keeping the spinnaker halyard under control is this "squirrel cage" roller that winds the excess*

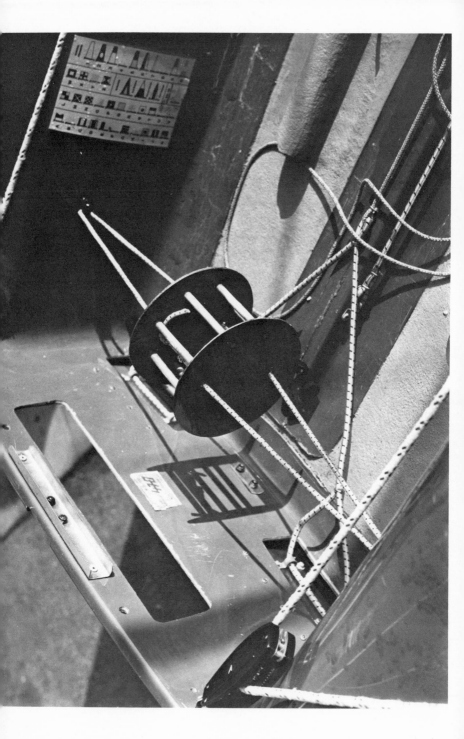

satisfactory. The halyard leads back through a jamb cleat *in front* of the fairlead eye, so it jams automatically (see Figure 8). The tail can be attached to a piece of shock cord so it disappears from the cockpit.

Sheets: We use ⅜-inch line on both our main and jib sheets. I think it's a good idea, if you use a large jib sheet, to splice a smaller line (about a quarter inch) to the end so that you won't have such a huge knot in the clew of the jib. Make as many lines as you can into a continuous loop; both jib and spinnaker sheets should definitely be continuous. On the mainsheet, we use wire block hangers to lower the boom blocks and reduce the amount of sheet needed (see Figure 10). On the 470, we use a lever yang that gets us an effective 16:1 power ratio and little stretch.

Centerboard: We use a shock cord to hold the centerboard down and a 4:1 purchase on the "up" line which leads to the skipper. The shock cord doesn't pull the board down, but it will hold it in place once it's been pulled down. I usually just grab the shock cord and yank the board down. With the 4:1 up line, I can pull the board up while sitting on the rail, which is important as you round the weather mark. I can even pull it up as we drive upwind in a lot of wind to ease weather helm, which saves having to luff up to trim the boat for heavy air. Be sure that the purchases on the centerboard are strongly anchored. We tore the front of the centerboard well off twice with the 4:1 tackle, so now we use the mast as an anchor.

When rigging (or re-rigging) the boat, decide early what should lead back to the skipper. Too many people lead everything back, but they shouldn't. If you have barber haulers, the crew can handle them even on a trapeze boat. The same holds true for the spinnaker pole downhaul and the topping lift. By the same token, anything that has to be adjusted while going to weather in a trapeze boat should lead to the skipper.

Our topping lift is wire, which leads to a rope tail and a cleat on the centerboard well. The downhaul is shock cord, with a rope backup so that it can be cinched down positively in heavy wind to

Figure 10 ▪

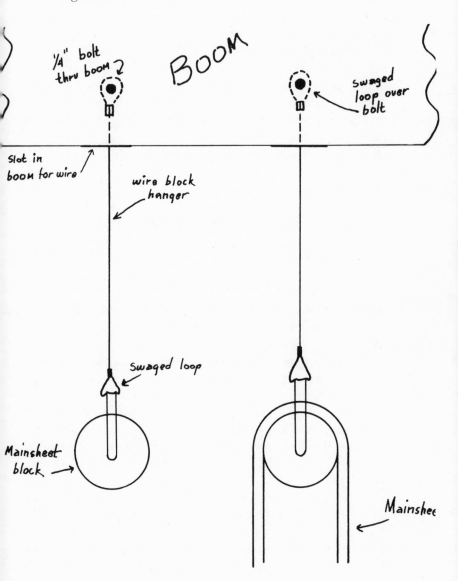

prevent the pole from skying up. Both the lift and downhaul are attached to one snap clip that hooks into an eye on the pole. My crew likes having a snap clip instead of a hook; it takes longer to set but it's absolutely positive.

Most people assume that the spinnaker sheet lead should be led as far aft and as far outboard as possible. That's not always true. Our 470 leads are a bit forward on the stern so that the spinnaker sheet doesn't override the boom, which is quite short.

For jib leads, we use a ratchet block plus an attached jamb cleat. The 470 has such a small jib that you really don't need a ratchet block, but it improves our communications. I can tell my crew to bring in the jib two clicks easier and more accurately than if I say half an inch.

The main thing in rigging your deck layout is to keep everything as simple as possible. Don't get so involved in adding additional purchase to your rigging that you actually start adding friction. Lead the essential items to the skipper and let the crew handle the rest. That's what he's along to do.

I have short legs and don't like to hike, but I certainly will if I have to. On the other hand, no trapeze boat should have hiking straps for the crew. You won't use them if you're sailing effectively, and they clutter up the boat.

To improve the crew's footing on the rail, I use wet suit material glued down with epoxy. It's very secure and it doesn't do major damage to pants and knees like sand or gravel. The 470 class didn't like it when we appeared at the world's championship in Montreal with a laced rope through the rail for improved footing, and they promptly declared it illegal. If you can, use the laced rope or, best of all, put toe straps on the rail for the crew's feet.

I see people using heavy shock cord on trapeze returns. That's silly. It's only intended to keep the trapeze wire handy. Too strong cord can pull the crew off balance or restrict his movements. Use a light shock cord. Most trapeze handles are far too low; the crew ends up doing pull-ups all day long. When your

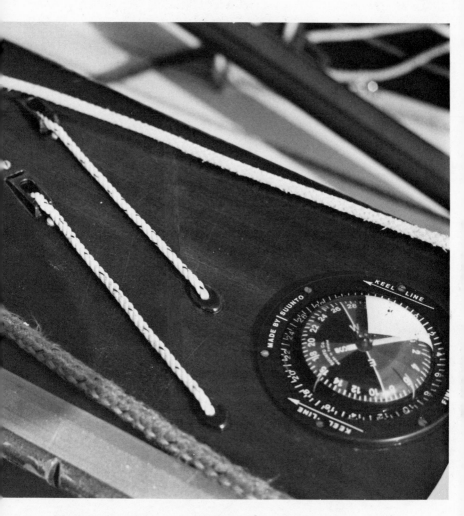

Figure 11 ■ *Keeping the deck simple is important in a small boat. This FD solved the problem of extra lines by leading them back into the deck with shock cord to keep tension on the excess.*

crew is hooked up on the low trapeze ring, he should just be able to reach the handle. In that way, the crew can swing out with a straight arm after a tack and then hook up. Remember that a trapeze crew has two responsibilities: to get out on the wire and to pull in the jib. My 470 crew hooks up *after* he's cleated the jib; he holds himself on the wire one-handed by the trapeze handle. It's easier than it sounds if the lengths are right.

Figure 12 ■ *One step more complicated than the standard "dumb-bell" shaped trapeze hook is the adjustable arrangement shown here. The jamb cleat allows the crew to support his weight while adjusting the exact height.*

PRE-RACE: HULL PREPARATION

Chapter **3**

ONCE YOU'VE CHOSEN and purchased your boat, start work on the hull which, whether you bought new or used, is certain to need it. I turn the boat over and chock it solidly with wedges and carpeting. Starting with 240-grit wet-or-dry sandpaper on a *long* sanding block, I knock off the bulges or lumps in the hull. Few hulls are really smooth when you get them. Be sure to use a sanding block at least the full length of the sandpaper. After working the bottom over to remove the high spots, I switch to 400 wet-or-dry for a fairly hard sanding. The final step is with 600 wet-or-dry to finish off the hull.

At this point, you've probably got a pretty smooth hull, but don't wax it! Wax measurably slows a finely sanded hull. The best finishing procedure is to buff the hull out by hand with just a rag—don't even use rubbing compound—to get the sticky fiberglass or paint dust off.

If your boat has a centerboard gasket; you should fill in the space around it (and the screw holes) with Bondo or fiberglass resin and microballoons for smoothness. We've started using a Mylar flap with 4-ounce Ripstop nylon tape on it, and it's just great. It doesn't tear or fray, and it lasts forever. We overlap the two flaps by a minimum of an eighth of an inch (but no more than one quarter inch). We also cut an opening at the back of the well to let the trapped water drain out (see Figure 13). This should be a vee about two inches long, tapering forward and with the widest end aft.

Before we started opening the back of the well flap, the water in the centerboard well sometimes overflowed out of the trunk into the boat. That meant that we were always dragging along

⅛" to ¼" OVERLAP

Figure 13 ▪

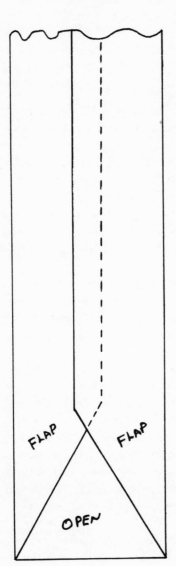

2 INCHES

about ten pounds of useless water inside the trunk, and it was annoying to slosh around ankle deep in the boat.

I like the Elvstrom bailers, and any class boat that allows bailers should certainly have them. I don't find much effect on us from drag when we sail, even when they're down. But if you have bailers on both sides of the centerboard well (as you should), *never* have both of them down at the same time. That sets up a bubble flow along each side of the boat and your rudder becomes much less effective. You can feel the difference very suddenly, so put one bailer down at a time. As a final reminder on hull smoothness, any aperture on the bottom should be as smooth as possible, regardless of whether it's big or little.

If we're involved in a major regatta, we'll use 600 wet-or-dry halfway through the series. It's amazing how much dirt the boat can pick up, so we use the sandpaper just like a cleanser. As a matter of fact, it's a good idea to use the sandpaper before the regatta too; it takes off the sticky residue that you pick up on the road. We don't sand the hull much above the waterline, since you shouldn't sail the boat with very much heel.

As far as finishes go, I don't believe in using any on a fiberglass boat. I've experimented with polymers some, but I wasn't really pleased with the results. I understand now that you need perfectly clean water for polymers to be effective, because pollution of several types can set the polymer off and create a sticky hull.

I've also never used graphite coatings on the hull, but I think they're great on the centerboard and rudder. The graphite finish forces you to keep the surfaces finely sanded, and the board and rudder are really critical for drag.

We used a Teflon coating on a Snipe for a while when Teflon was the rage. It was really effective for about a month, and then it seemed to be worse than paint. Once the Teflon is leached out of the paint solution, you're left with a rough and porous coating. Fiberglass, if it is well filled and has a good gel surface, is as effective as anything.

If I had a wood hull, I'd use either a graphite paint or a two-part catalyst paint. The harder the paint, the better it can be sanded out for maximum smoothness. I don't like varnished hulls for just that reason: they never seem to get really hard. You can always stick your fingernail into the surface or peel it back. That isn't good enough. Catalytic varnish like Laminar XL-500 was really good on one of my Snipes for a couple of years, but that's really just a clear paint and not a varnish. The drawback to it was that it was tough to work with. We had to spray it on and it would run and it was just too much effort.

Centerboards and rudders, as I said before, are *really* critical. Much of your work should be on the underwater surfaces. But since each class needs something slightly different, the best bet is to check what's going well in that particular class. Take a good look at the class rules and see if there might be an improvement to be made, a not unlikely happening if you approach the class with an open mind.

Thickness in both board and rudder is important. The centerboard should always be as thick as class rules allow. The rudder doesn't have to be maximum thickness, but there are always exceptions to both rules.

I'm not a flow engineer, but boards and rudders are nowhere near the optimum for performance. It seems that a ratio of 5 to 1 for length vs. thickness is what you're looking for. This means that a 12-inch long rudder should be more than two inches thick (ideally).

With a jibing board, I don't think you can get away with more than about 2½ degrees of jibe. Most classes seem to respond best with 1 to 1½ degrees. And in nearly every class that allows a jibing centerboard, it is absolutely imperative to have it. You won't win without it. In the 470, jibing boards never really caught on because of the strange board shape. Half of the board, by class rules, had to be flat so it stalls very easily. As we were writing this book, I was the only one with a jibing 470 board in the U.S., and it has since been prohibited. We induced jibe by blocking the back of the board and letting the front flop around. Our block was a thin fiberglass batten glassed onto each side of the board. It seems that in Lidos, Coronado-15s, International-14s, 505s, and FDs, you can hardly race without a jibing board. You end up going higher to weather and no slower by having the jibing board, so it's a simple choice: win or lose. With a jibing board, you may gain 20–30 lengths on one leg of the course alone. In a lot of chop, the jibing board frankly isn't too good because it stalls so easily, but if your board is thick enough you can sometimes get away with it.

To get rid of the jibing action when we didn't need it (such as in chop), we just tightened down on the pivot bolt so the well was compressed and that automatically limited the board. It made it quite a bit more difficult to raise the board, but I can live with that. As example of the value of a jibing board, we were obviously faster at the 1974 CORK in smooth water. In one smooth water race in eight knots of wind, we went from 50th place to second place . . . mainly because of being able to sail higher and just as fast as everyone else.

But a jibing board can also hurt you in some conditions. At the 470 Worlds in Italy, it hurt me when it was choppy (which was most of the time!). The boat didn't seem to have any punch until one day that there was smooth water, then we were off and gone. So you have to decide again on what you want, and then take the consequences.

In the Coronado-15, you are permitted by the rules to have a total of one-quarter inch of jibe, but it doesn't have to be divided evenly on each tack. We thought about that for a while and then took the whole quarter inch and put it on the starboard tack side, which is like having half an inch on an evenly divided board. It gave us a jibe angle of about three degrees and we were absolutely untouchable on starboard tack. We were neutral on port, so some boats were better than us on that tack. But we'd thought about the situation beforehand. You very rarely sail alongside anyone on port tack. Nobody ever tacks onto your lee bow while you're on port tack. You rarely start on port. And you don't often approach the weather mark on port except when you're alone. So it's not too important to have a lot of lifting action on port tack. When we put the whole jibe angle on starboard, nobody (and I mean *nobody*) could lee bow us because they would have to tack well to weather to hold us back. We could always lift away from the fleet at the start. And we were always in great shape approaching a weather mark or finish line. It was incredible! We haven't done it to any other boat, but just because the situation hasn't seemed as good. Just remember that a jibing board really helps. . . . it only takes a few minutes of sailing several degrees higher than the rest of the fleet and you're long gone.

A maximum thickness board will stall much later than a thin board, just because of the basic hydrodynamics of its shape. For smooth lakes, I'd use a narrow board if you don't need too much jibe action. If you intend to have some centerboard jibe, then a thick board is necessary so that you won't always be stalled out.

. Most boats, where the choice of shape is open, are using a laminar shape, with the maximum thickness about ⅓ back from the leading edge followed by a flat taper aft and an elliptical leading edge.

Perhaps it is appropriate to add a word here about stalling, which is a concept that most people don't understand completely. Stall is that point at which water no longer flows evenly past each side of the centerboard or rudder. The water becomes turbulent on one side or the other, and speed is dragged down by this suction. It's as simple as that, but it causes airplanes to fall out of the sky and sailboats to fall behind in races. So you should take great pains to insure that the flow past your underwater fins is as smooth, or laminar, as possible.

Since a sailboat makes leeway, the underwater fins are forced to drag through the water at a slight angle (except when running) and this is an important point to remember: every centerboard and rudder is *always* sailing in a stalled condition. It is the *degree* of that stall that is critical. For that reason, a jibing centerboard, with its built-in angle, has more stall at the outset than a board that is parallel with the centerline of the boat.

You've probably experienced stall but been too busy to recognize it. For example, you may have pulled the rudder hard to weather in an attempt to duck behind a boat in front of you . . . only to find your boat continuing straight ahead. Your rudder had stalled and was no longer effective at turning your boat. For that reason, you should steer with as little rudder motion as possible. By the same token, a short fat rudder (or board) will maintain a laminar flow longer than a flat plate.

Our 470 board and rudder are eight-piece cross-laminated spruce with a layer of airplane glass and the gelcoat over that. Ours are very near the minimum class weight since centerboards are like masts—you need to keep them as light as possible to reduce the pendulum effect in chop.

A lot of people think that a centerboard should be heavy like a keel, to help hold you upright. That's true, but only if you're

Figure 14 ■

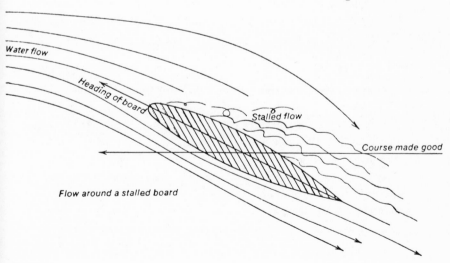

Water flow

Heading of board

Stalled flow

Course made good

Flow around a stalled board

heeled over. If you're heeling, then you're going slowly because the boat is off its lines. So keep the boat flat and the board light. That's especially true of rudders, which should absolutely be as light as possible to keep the weight out of the end of the boat.

Don't try for too sharp a trailing edge. Our centerboard tapers back as though it were going to a very sharp edge, but it ends in a $^1/_{16}$-inch flat section on the trailing edge. Sharp trailing edges may be slightly faster as long as they are perfect, but when they get even a tiny ding, they become very slow. The flat edge doesn't seem to be as affected by dings, as well as being hard to chip in the first place. The flat trailing edge can stand burrs much better without losing speed, and just think of the pounding the board takes when you yank it up suddenly.

In most classes, the pivot point should be as far aft as possible. Where there are tolerances, put the pivot point far back in the well and close to the leading edge of the board. It seems that in most boats the centerboards are never far enough aft for heavy winds. You get weather helm very early, as a result. In fact, in the 470 we sail upwind in a blow with the board up halfway to move its center of resistance farther aft to relieve the helm. Flying Dutchmen and 505s are lucky that they can move the entire pivot assembly aft in heavy air or forward in light, but the rest of the strict classes have to live with exploiting the tolerances early and then relying on angling the board back in a breeze.

In extremely light air, you should angle your board slightly forward to give yourself a little weather helm. The unfortunate thing about weather helm is that you can get it easily by heeling the boat, but you can't get rid of it in strong winds by keeping the boat flat. Weather helm doesn't make you any faster—in fact it slows you up with drag—but it makes your sailing easier and gives you a feel for wind and wave. If you can sail without any weather helm at all and still honestly keep the boat hard on the wind, then you'll have an advantage. But it's a rare person who can do that.

I always feel better when I have a little bit of weather helm.

It takes perfect concentration to sail fast with no helm, so you can't look away from the jib for even a second. With a little pull from the tiller, you can look away at the course or your competitors and not find yourself inadvertently far off the wind.

In fact, I used to practice when I was younger (and still do occasionally) by blindfolding myself (with a crew aboard!) and then sailing for half an hour. It's easier to just close your eyes, but I tend to cheat on that. Sailing blindfolded is especially good when you're trying to get acclimated to a new boat. When you are forced to sail without any visual indications, you have to rely on feel and touch. You get to know your boat better, and it seems to help when you're trying a new sail—you can actually "feel" a good sail easier than you can decide by looking at it. Without visuals, you can also get a much clearer idea of the effect the centerboard position has on the amount of weather helm you have.

Rudders should have basically the same shape as the centerboard, although they are often thicker. Again, it depends upon your own steering technique. If you're a hard steerer and you work the tiller a lot, then you should have a maximum thickness rudder to prevent the rudder from stalling. If you tend to find a groove and not steer too much, then a minimum thickness rudder is fine. I tend to do a little of both, depending upon the particular situation, so I usually have maximum thickness rudders. In that way I'm safe, since the extra drag of thickness is not as great as a continually stalling rudder.

The majority of my sailing is in the ocean, and you do a lot of steering there . . . over and around waves. Be sure that the rudder is strong but light, since it takes a lot of strain from constant use as well as the side loads of planing.

In the Lido-14, our centerboard and rudder are basically the same shape as in the 470, but we're less conscious of weight since it's a much smaller part of the 310-pound total weight of the Lido. And we usually sail in smooth bay waters, so the pitching effect of a heavy rudder isn't as important.

In the Snipe, the centerboard is a big flat plate of aluminum

Figure 15 ■

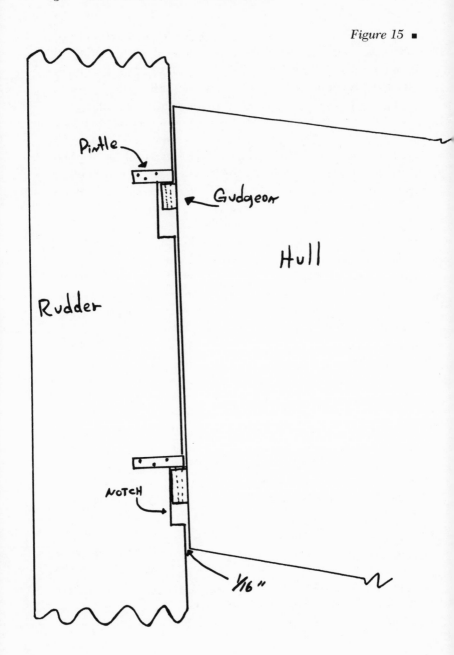

Pintle

Gudgeon

Hull

Rudder

NOTCH

1/16"

or steel, and the rudder is wood. With the plate, we round the front edge almost to a radius and taper the back to a flat spot. We're not too concerned about an efficient shape since it's so terrible already. The main problem is vibration, which I think slows you down. It seems to be a waste of energy, although some sailors say the vibration is permissible. I don't agree and, besides, it's annoying as hell.

Snipe rudders have been made up to 1⅞ inches thick, but I use a 1½-inch thickness for normal sailing or 1¼ inches on lakes. A Snipe really has to be steered a lot because it's so unresponsive, so a fat rudder is probably a good idea.

The distance from the rudder to the transom should be absolutely minimum; almost touching is best. There's no reason to have any gap there. Water comes off the hull, re-forms, and then breaks again. If you can reduce or eliminate that, you're cutting a lot of turbulence. That option is available on the Snipe, but not on too many other boats. In the Snipe, we recessed the pintles into the rudder itself so the space is less than $1/16$ of an inch (see Figure 15). By the same token, you have to get it really close before you cut the turbulence, so if you have some separation, a little more probably won't hurt.

If you have kick-up rudders, sail with them fully down. The only exception to that is something the Europeans have started doing in the 470 class. They cock the rudder blade up at 20–30 degrees before the start. That gives them a much more effective steering control, and you can really lever the boat into and out of holes between other boats. It's probably illegal, but it sure helps. As soon as the gun goes off and they're moving, they yank the rudder right down again anyway.

The tiller should be both light and strong for the same reasons as the rudder. The connection of the tiller to the rudder should be really snug also. I think the tiller should move up or down on every boat, so that when you're planing, you can move aft and still get the tiller over your knees. Otherwise your control is limited as you come off a big wave. Surprisingly, you don't see this often in the 470 class, but we made a special rudder head that permitted it and it works beautifully.

The only reason I can see for using a telescoping tiller extension is if you're going to give the helm to the crew. We're trying out a technique where my crew moves aft on the wire as we near the weather mark. I pass him the long tiller extension and then he steers while I set the spinnaker pole. We find that we can do it in up to 18 knots of wind and it helps keep his weight well out on the wire where it does the most good. And my weight inboard doesn't hurt us as much as the crew coming off the trapeze would hurt us.

That brings us to a good point to end this section on. My weight doesn't help or hinder our racing as some people's weight might. If it doesn't really matter, then I feel that I might as well be comfortable, so I don't hike hard at all. For that reason, I don't need a long tiller extension and I don't worry as much about hiking straps. We've experimented with me fully hiked versus not hiking at all, and it just didn't seem to make any difference. So you have to take some of my thoughts on equipment with a grain of salt, as well as using the same reasoning on your own sailing style. If, hiking out doesn't help you but tires you out, then don't do it.

SAILS

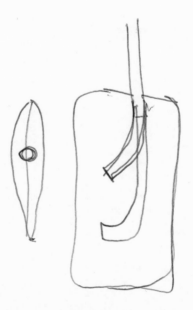

Chapter 4

BEING A SAILMAKER, I have a lot of definite ideas about sails, but this is going to be a short chapter because my ideas concern the actual making of sails rather than what we'll discuss here, which is the use of your sails. Despite what some other books say, the majority of decisions should always be made by your sailmaker. He's a professional, so trust his judgment.

A person starting out in a new class should look around and see what sails are winning. Analyze that information: are those sails winning because they are fast, or is it because they're the only sail out there? For example, our sails are winning a lot in the Lido-14 class. But they are also the most-often-used sails by far. So it's a circle. They win a lot so they are used a lot. When that happens to a dominant degree, then I wouldn't even question it; those are the sails to buy. That's an easy example, particularly because they're my sails, but it applies to all classes: buy what is fast.

In a class like the Snipe, where you see winners using Norths, Ullmans, Murphy & Nyes, and other sails, don't go by the straight results. See who will give you the best service in your area. Always try to buy locally so that you can get some mileage out of your sail dollar in service and attention.

I don'. believe in sails being cut for a certain area, at least not in the one-design classes. Not that there aren't different wind conditions, but class racing forces you to travel outside your own area. If your area is remarkably different, such as San Francisco with its wind and chop, then you should tell the sailmaker that, but don't expect to do well when you race in a light-air area. I'm convinced that a sailor will win far more often with one good set of all-around sails then he ever will with different suits of sails for different conditions. For one thing, you get used to working with that one set and you learn to change its shape to suit your needs at that time. If you have to make a choice between light and heavy suits of sails, you're bound to make the wrong choice fairly often. So I'd recommend getting one good set of sails and learning to use them. The money you save can be used to replace them more frequently.

Don't ever make demands on a sailmaker. What really irritates me, and unfortunately I get it all the time, is someone coming to me for a sail in a class where my sails are already doing well and telling me how to cut the sail. That might be acceptable if I'd never made a sail for that class, but if I'm building sails that are winning, then it's best to let me make the best sail I can. If you don't like what the sailmaker is currently producing for that class, then go somewhere else. Don't try to change the sailmaker. Put your faith in him; he wants you to win with his label, so he can't afford to make a bad sail.

You'll probably have some options, in any case. For Snipes, we're making two mainsails, with light and heavy cloth. We make a light, full jib and a so-called normal jib. For the 470, we make two totally different sets of sails depending upon the choice of mast. In the 470, the jib and spinnaker are the same, but the mainsails are changed to fit either a bendy or a stiff spar.

In Snipes, we try to encourage buying an all-purpose main and two jibs. That may seem contradictory to what I said about having just one set of sails, but the Snipe is pretty critical. You need the extra push of a special full jib in light airs. If you can have two jibs in a class, you always seem to need a light jib rather than an extra heavy jib, especially in light-air lakes.

Once you've received your new sails, if they don't look right, go back. You paid a bundle and that entitles you to some time with the sailmaker. Often he can give you advice on setting your sails over the phone, but sometimes it's worth the effort to take your boat down and rig it in his parking lot and look at the sails.

There's a lot of talk about sails becoming obsolete as shapes change. That change takes place differently in various classes, and even in the same class the rate changes at times. In the 470, we've changed our mainsail pattern thirty times in the last five years. We haven't changed the jib at all. In the Lido-14, we change the patterns about once a year. That's because you're only allowed one new sail a year and so we don't think it's fair to update more often.

Our Snipe patterns haven't changed in a long time, because the Snipe has been around so long that the days of experimentation are past and the sail shapes have settled down.

In the 470, you can only use one set of sails per regatta, which means you have to use the same main and jib for the whole series regardless of the weather. In Snipes, I take one main and two jibs to an event. As a sailmaker, I could easily take sails for every possible weather condition, but I'm like a lot of sailors. If I give myself more choices, I seem to get confused and always put the wrong sail up. So I keep my choices to a minimum and use a simple, all-purpose set of sails in my boats.

If you're really serious about winning, plan to get a new set of sails at least once a season. The sailcloth is good for six or seven times that period, but the shape changes and the cloth becomes more porous (and therefore slower). In fact, I think that after five regattas you can detect a slowing that might be worth six boat lengths a race. That's not much, but it's more than I'm willing to give away freely. For that reason, I think it's a good idea to get a new set of sails before a major event. The old wives' tale that sails have to be broken in before they assume the correct shape might have been true of cotton sails, but it's no longer valid. A sail is the correct shape as it comes from the sailmaker . . . ready to win.

I discourage recutting old sails because you spend about as much money as on a new set and you still have old cloth which is porous and slow because the finish and filler of the cloth have disappeared and the old cloth stretches more.

Never leave your sails in the sun or in a hot place like the trunk of a car; you'll bake the life out of them. The heat causes the synthetic fibers to break down quickly. Don't leave your sails up at the dock to flog; that fatigues the fibers and encourages the sails to stretch unnecessarily. Rinse your sails off after contact with salt or polluted water, and always fold them after use. Rolling the sails is even better than folding, because every fold damages fibers. Don't ever wash sails with anything but clear water. One of my Lido-14 customer's wife took the brand new set of sails home and, to surprise her husband, promptly washed and dried them, which made them as soft and limp as ten-year-old sails.

A lot of people use battens that are far too flexible. The batten is used to hold the leech of the sail out, so stiffness is desirable. The only place a flexible batten is needed is on the top batten, which extends for such a distance across the width of the sail that it has to bend considerably.

In small boats, the spherical cut spinnaker (horizontal panels of cloth) seems faster than a radial-head chute (with some vertical panels). The spherical produces a flatter spinnaker with more shoulder to it, which gives more projected area without adding depth. As a spherical gets older, it becomes flatter, which is quite acceptable. The radial spinnaker just doesn't seem as fast in small boats, and it's harder to keep flying.

The last item in this section is one of the most important: yarn on the sail. We put just a single piece of yarn near the jib luff and none on the mainsail. The jib yarn serves as an indication if I'm sailing too high or too low while on the wind. Yarn on the mainsail just doesn't seem to work. Most people don't realize that yarn on a mainsail (of a sloop) isn't supposed to work like on a jib. When you're sailing efficiently, both yarns will stream aft on the jib. If both yarns stream aft on the mainsail, your mainsail will be too far out; it's undersheeted. The windward yarn should always be slightly folding forward if the slot between the main and jib is working properly.

MASTS AND RIGGING

Chapter **5**

THE FINN was probably the last modern class to hold out on
going to aluminum masts, and now nearly everyone is using the
metal mast quite successfully. I think that if you could get really
good quality wood as well as a craftsman who knew what he was
doing, you could build a better mast. But given today's conditions, aluminum is the only answer. Besides, it's far easier to
maintain.

Aluminum spars have become much more sophisticated,
especially now that manufacturers don't have to weld the taper
into them. A number of manufacturers are twisting the extrusions
or compressing them to achieve the taper, which is much neater
than before. The popular French Z-Spar 470 masts are beautifully
weld-free.

Obviously, each class needs a different spar, but there is one
basic rule to follow always. You want a mast that stays straight
sideways until you can't keep the boat flat, and then you want the
tip to bend off to leeward to ease heeling force. The same applies
to fore-and-aft bend: you want the mast as straight as possible
until you can't keep the boat flat, and then it should bend as low
as possible to take the draft out of the sail.

There shouldn't be much aft bend in the top half of the mast,
because that forces the sailmaker to put too much luff curve into
the mainsail and then the rig won't be fast in light or medium
airs. If you put luff curve down low to match the potential bend
down low, when the mast bends in fresh air it sucks draft out of
the sail. So you have a combination that is good in a whole spec-
trum of wind conditions. A second point in favor of bending down

low is that it opens the leech at the top of the sail; it seems to be very important to have good draft and an open leech in the top of the mainsail.

I use two different masts for my 470: an Elvstrom and a Z-Spar. The Z-Spar is good in lots of chop and the Elvstrom is good in more normal conditions. Each spar has its own characteristics: the Z-Spar is flexible fore-and-aft and very stiff sideways, while the Elvstrom is stiff fore-and-aft and bends sideways easily. The Z-Spar gives much more power to punch through chop because you can flatten the sail by bending the mast. If I need sailshape rather than outright power, the Elvstrom is best.

In the Snipe, we're using the Cobra mast, which bends fore-and-aft up high and sideways along the whole length. I think the old Proctor "E" section was better, but you can't get them anymore.

Any time you can, you should step the mast on the keel; it gives you a control point at the deck to restrict or induce bend. Step the mast as low on the keel as you can, especially if you have a long mast, because it increases your leverage immensely.

If you pre-load your spreaders so that their tips are forward of the shroud's normal straight line downward, you reduce the bend in the mast. If you load your spreader aft of the straight line, you encourage bend. Just imagine that your shroud will be straight when you're out sailing: if the spreader is pre-loaded, the shroud will pull the spreader and thus the mast aft. For example, in the Z-Spar mast you put the spreader aft of the shroud by about 1½ inches because you want the mast to bend to flatten the sail.

In the 470, the mainsail I use with the Elvstrom mast has almost no luff curve, so a straight spar is a necessity. Therefore, I load the spreader forward of the shroud. In light breezes, I don't set my shroud tension too tight, which keeps the mast straight by itself. As the wind comes up, I tighten the shroud tension to force the mast to stay straight. The spreaders are just pulling the middle of the mast back into a straight line.

With the Z-Spar, I reverse the process. In light wind and

chop, I set the shrouds up very tightly to force six or seven inches of bend, which matches the luff curve of the sail. As the wind comes up and the mast wants to bend even more, I ease off the shrouds to maintain the same amount of bend. Basically the spreaders are used to force each mast to assume the best shape for the mainsail.

On the Snipe, we try to keep the mast very straight until we're unable to hike enough to hold the boat flat. Snipes are tough to keep down, so we start bending the mast at about 12 knots of wind. Our spreaders swing freely, but they're blocked aft to stop swinging when the tips are about 24 inches apart (when both are swept aft). That amount seemsto keep the mast from turning the mainsail completely inside-out.

I think any boat without a spinnaker should be sailed with loose rigging so the mast can be pushed forward downwind. Spinnaker boats should be sailed tight. When I tune a non-spinnaker boat, I set the shrouds so that the mast is about plumb for downwind speed, and then I allow either the headstay or the jib halyard to rake the mast aft until I have a slight weather helm when the boat is being sailed flat in 10–12 knots of wind.

On a spinnaker boat, I snug the mast down at whatever the rake is that gives me the slight weather helm when going to weather. Having the mast go forward or plumb doesn't seem to help once you get the spinnaker up.

Some sailors go to a lot of effort to streamline their spreaders, but I've always used just standard off-the-shelf spreaders. But then, I've never been too concerned about wind resistance. One thing to be certain of, though, is that the spreaders should be strong and stiff enough so they will never break.

The type of mast you have is going to directly affect the type of halyard locks you use. The only excuse for having a halyard lock in the first place is to reduce the bending forces on the mast and to keep your mast tight. If you look at the diagram (Figure 16), you can see that a halyard that goes up and over the top of the mast acts like a bow on an arrow, in this case the arrow being

Figure 16 ■ *In this exaggerated diagram, note the distance that the jib halyard block and the masthead (main halyard sheave) are lowered by mast bend. Without a halyard lock, both the jib and the main on the bending mast would be loose and misshapen as the halyard was eased by the mast bend.*

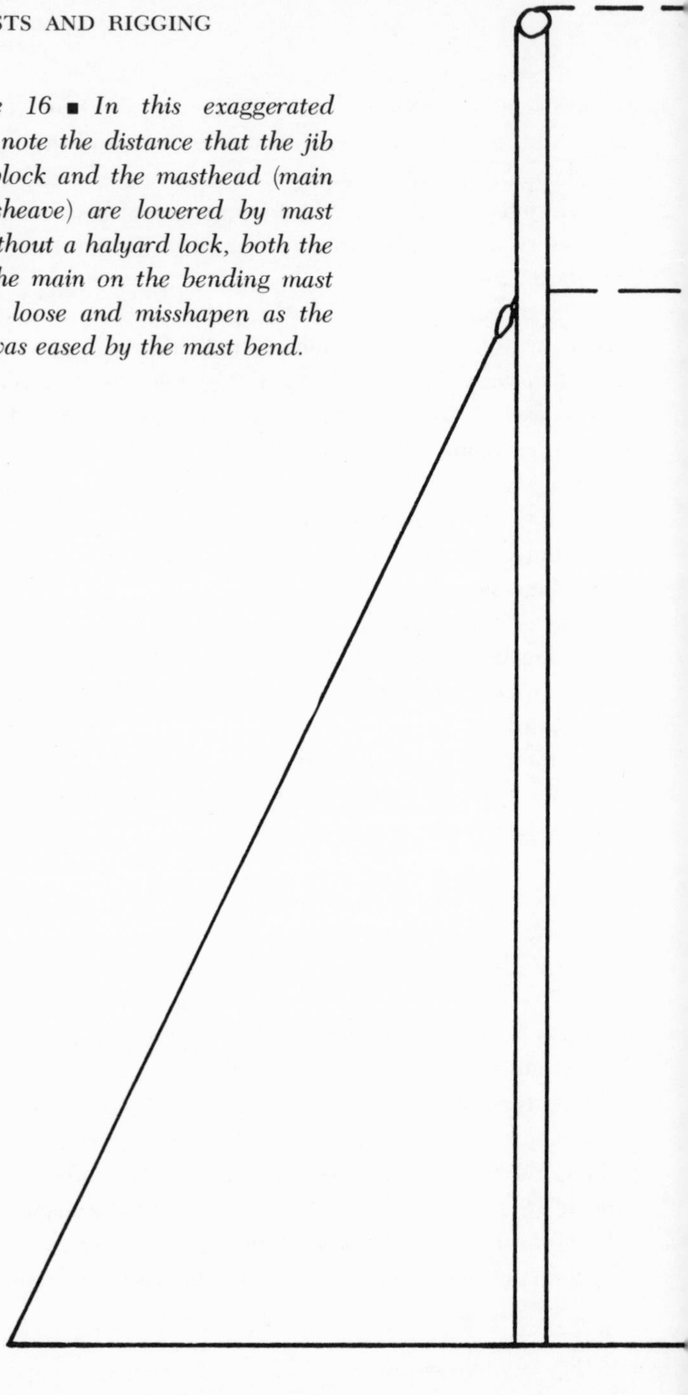

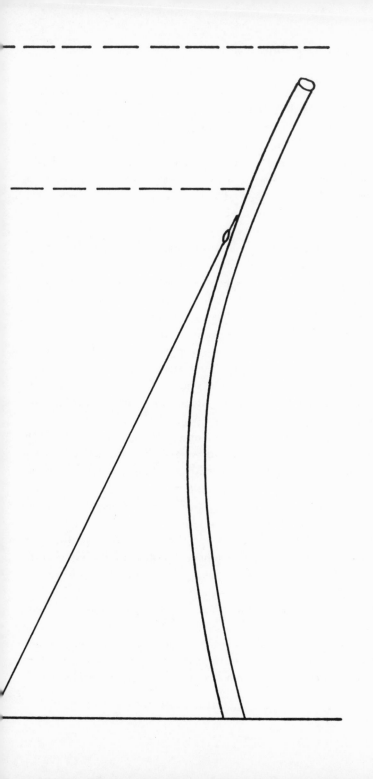

a mast. Since the mast can't shoot through the bottom of the boat (you hope!), it will bend. A halyard lock reduces that load by half. It also permits you to keep your halyard tight even if the mast does bend, since mast bend will shorten the distance between the halyard cleat and the halyard block (see diagram). Our Elvstrom 470 mast is never supposed to bend much, so we don't use a lock at all. But because of the bend of the Z-Spar, we use a halyard lock at the masthead.

On the Snipe, I've used halyard locks but I don't use one now since the halyard is internal. If your spar is a real noodle and you have external halyards, be sure you have a lock at the top.

I don't recommend having a lock on the jib halyard. It's really critical to be able to adjust the luff tension and/or mast rake, so I always run the jib halyard down to either a purchase drum or a tackle arrangement so it can be changed easily.

The position of the shroud chainplate is sometimes left optional, as in the Snipe class, for instance. In the Snipe, we've moved our chainplate outboard and aft for most conditions. In very light airs, you can move the shroud inboard and forward, which allows you to ease your boom farther out on the runs. It doesn't seem to matter much going upwind either way. The only problem with moving a shroud position forward and inboard is that you'll probably lose your mast over the bow when it blows hard. If you sail regularly in smooth water and light air, move the shroud in and forward, but because we sail in stronger winds and lots of chop, we have only the one out and aft chainplate, but we solved most of the problem of the shroud not allowing the main to go out on the run. Since we have a push-pull mast raker in the Snipe, we just don't let the mast go fully upright, which leaves the shroud slightly loose and the boom can swing freely.

Speaking of booms, they should be as light and as stiff as possible. I don't like bendy booms at all. A rectangular boom seems to be the strongest, provided the wall is thick enough. Snipes went through a period of having tall thin "plank" booms, but they would turn inside-out on reaches and they were always breaking.

As I mentioned before, you have much more control with a stern traveler, but in some classes like the 470 and 505, you sheet so hard and have so much mast rake that the boom is right on the stern deck. So a stern traveler wouldn't work. In fact, in heavy air the boom is often below the deck level, either inside the cockpit or outside the rail. The problem with sheeting down inside the cockpit is that if you ever get a knockdown, you can't ease the traveler because the boom won't go beyond the hull side. Then you're in real trouble.

Ideally, I think the inhaul system is better than an adjustable outhaul. That fastens the clew at the maximum outboard position and tension is taken by moving the tack toward the mast. It gives you the maximum area away from the mast disturbance, and it eliminates all the rigging on the boom. In the 470, we have a lever that releases the outhaul about two inches. That makes a big difference off the wind, but some people overlook it. Actually, our outhaul is double-ended (see Figure 17) with a jamb cleat for fine adjustments.

I'm relaxed about windage. I try to fair most spar fittings in with microballoons, but I won't sacrifice anything for windage. If I can reduce windage just by fairing, fine. But I won't eliminate a fitting just for that purpose.

On the 470, I run the shrouds into holes in the mast side and then bolt them through internally. It's much cleaner than using tangs. But I don't really worry about windage on the Snipe, because the boat is so slow and you can't use all of its power in most cases anyway. The 470 is light and underpowered, so windage is important. At the 1974 470 world's championship in Naples, the Italian coach suggested that I get my hair cut to decrease my personal windage, but I thought that was going a bit too far.

Except for class rules, there is absolutely no reason for any boat to have external halyards. Running them inside is a free reduction in windage, so do it.

I don't think most small boats need diamonds or jumpers;

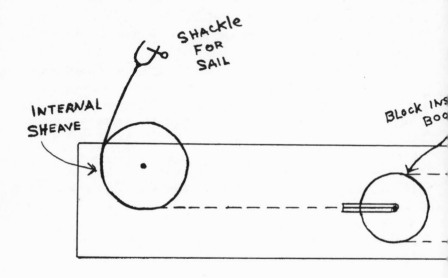

Figure 17 ■ *Interval 2:1 Outhaul.*

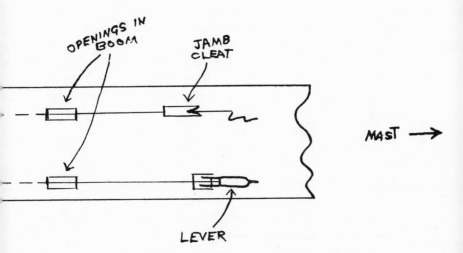

Lever releases large amount of outhaul cleat for fine tuning

that's an indication of a poorly designed rig being used improperly. The Thistle and Lido both have diamonds as a class requirement, but a single spreader rig would be more effective.

If you can change the height of the spreader above the deck, it's worth experimenting. Generally, the higher the spreader (up to a point), the better the control of your mast. Some boats, like the FD, have tried adjustable spreaders that can be moved while under sail. I think it's a great idea, but it just gets too complex. It would be nice to be able to set the rig up tight and then move the spreaders to bend or straighten the mast as needed. Maybe someone will come up with a simple way to achieve this.

I don't have a wind indicator on the top of my mast, only because I've never put it there. I have found that I am looking at the masthead flies on other boats. If I'm doing that, then I ought to have my own to watch. You should absolutely have yarn on the shrouds for reaching, but windward sailing should be done by watching the sails themselves.

A spinnaker pole should be stiff and easy to use. You're giving away power if it bends at all. The end fittings should lock on automatically, so the crew doesn't have to pull them open on the set. But they should be very positive in action. The trip line on our 470 pole is taped in the middle so that you can't accidentally release the wrong end on a jibe.

On the Snipe, we have two whisker poles—one long one for reaching when the jib should be out in front of the boat, and a short one for dead runs. I think two poles are easier than a collapsible pole; those always seem to collapse at the wrong moment.

A lot of people put a knot near the end of the spinnaker sheet so the spinnaker pole doesn't slip back. I think that's wrong, because you should be able to take the chute down with the pole still up and you can't do that when you have a knot. It may seem unusual, but there are a few occasions where you want to get rid of the spinnaker instantly to leeward, and just leave the pole up until later.

Most people, out of a sense of fear, make the trapeze wires too heavy. On the 470, we use $1/16$-inch 7 x 7 wire, which is plenty strong enough. It looks thin, but it breaks at about 700 pounds, and I don't think you'll ever have that big a crew. Don't use a wood handle (they break) and don't run the trapeze wire through the middle of a bar or rod for the handle. It chafes the crew's hands badly and it can even cut the soft skin between his fingers when they're wet. I like the open grip handle, and some kind of height adjustment is nice for the hook eye itself. Don't try to scrimp by using only a single ring on the trapeze wire. Use a dumbbell-shaped pair of rings or, at worst, a pair of separate rings connected by wire.

On our boat, the shock cord doesn't go directly to the bottom trapeze ring; it leads up to the handle first and then down to the ring. That keeps the rings off the deck and it holds the crew hooked up until he releases it as he swings in. We took the latch off Jack's trapeze harness because you can get into trouble trying to unhook it fast. With the open hook and the shock cord, he can flick off the trapeze wire with one hand, but it stays on otherwise.

Big trapeze boats, like Flying Dutchmen, need adjustments to let the crew go aft on reaches. Since the 470 is smaller, we find that having the two trapeze rings about twelve inches apart is sufficient to let the crew trapeze horizontally while on the wind and to be angled up slightly when we're on a reach so that he'll clear the water.

PRE-RACE: YOU

Chapter **6**

THERE IS A FINE LINE of difference between a *really* good sailor and just a good sailor. I think a lot of that difference is made up by the really good sailor in preparing himself mentally and physically for a race. The other sailor starts too late or shuts off too soon.

At a really important regatta—maybe one of three or four a year—my crew and I will sail steadily for about two weeks before the event, practicing tacks and jibes and checking sails and equipment. We stop sailing three days before we leave for the regatta, because we don't want to get stale and, besides, those three days give us a last chance to work on the boat and get packed.

We try to arrive at the location of the regatta several days before the first race. I like to spend two full days out on the water in the course area to check the weather, current, and the other items you need to know before racing. The last day before the series starts is our "one-hour" day. Usually there is a practice race, so that takes care of the hour practicing. We won't even sail the full practice race . . . we just sail the first few legs and then drop out, again to give ourselves a break.

To be very honest about physical conditioning, I'm not doing any. My 470 crew is running to improve his wind and his legs, and he's doing just a touch of weight-lifting. But I think it's more important to do "in-the-boat" conditioning than the straight physical workouts. Of course, it depends again on what you sail. Most two-man boats are not nearly as demanding as the single-handers. In the Snipe and 470, actual physical condition is not as critical as teamwork, agility, and coordination. If anything were

required, I'd say endurance would be most important, partic
larly in the crew.

Before a major regatta, I diet for two or three weeks. I ha
to lose fifteen to twenty pounds since I'm normally about 130 ar
I like to sail at about 110. I just can't do it quickly and keep r
strength, so it has to be a gradual loss.

When picking a crew, I look for two things and neither
sailing ability. I want a crew who has mental alertness. I'd defir
that as an overall sharpness and a high practical intelligence; I
always knows what is going on around him. But the main thing
look for is competitiveness. The good crew *has* to win. Tha
probably more important in the crew than in the skipper, b
cause the crew has little to do in much of the race. The skipp
has his own little projects to keep involved; steering, tactic
trim, etc. But the race isn't as exciting for the crew, who on
performs mechanical functions and sort of goes along for the rid
So it's tougher for a crew to stay psyched up for and during
race.

It's even more important that a crew do his job well whe
you're behind. He has to be able to say "all right, dammit, le
catch those guys." My regular 470 crew, Jack Jakosky, is the pe
fect example of that. He played pro basketball and I knew th
first time we sailed together that he'd be a great crew. Becau:
he just plain *had* to win.

On the race course, my crew doesn't get involved in de
cisions for the most part, and I think that's wise. Sometime
we discuss things, but not as a rule. Off the race course, he h
half the say in what rig or what sail we use.

The main reason we don't discuss things is that so mar
decisions have to be instantaneous. If you delay for a secono
you're in trouble. If you make a practice of being democratic an
always consulting your crew, you may hesitate when a cruci
decision comes along, and that's the end of your race. So don't I
too democratic.

The long-term decisions, such as which side of the course

favored, are always open for discussion. And before the start, we'll discuss our basic strategy for the race. But once we're on the race course, he just feeds me information about wind or other boats.

One huge problem is finding a crew that meets those qualifications and who is willing to commit himself for a long period of time. In our case, Jack committed more than two and a half years for trying for the 1976 Olympics. When you find a person with that much ambition, determination, and competitive spirit, he usually has his own boat.

One thing that really separates the average sailor from the great sailor is his crew. There's too much emphasis on getting a crew that has a lot of sailing ability. That can be taught. But having the same crew race after race gives you a definite advantage. You work together, think together, and react together. I'd much rather have a less talented crew regularly than a different "hotshot" in every race.

By the same token, don't expect to pick up a crew member today and start doing well tomorrow. I think it takes at least six months to train a good crew so that you work well as a team. Jack was an intercollegiate sailing champion, and it took us more than four months to start working well together.

Eliminating the spinnaker and trapeze makes crewing a lot easier. My wife, Betty, crews for me in the Lido-14 and, when it blows under fifteen knots, she does as well as anybody I've ever sailed with. She doesn't have the fierce drive that Jack has, but she's done it long enough to know the mechanics of jib trim and balance. In fact, she crewed for me when she was five years old and I was sailing an old Snowbird dinghy.

Early in the book, we discussed fitting a boat to your size and weight. Don't overlook size when you look for a crew. Pick someone who, combined with your own weight, is effective for that particular boat. Just for that very reason, I have different crews for my different boats.

I hear a lot about people "psyching up" before a race. I'm just not good at that. When we get to an event and we're practicing, I can tell if I'm going fast. If I'm going slowly, then I'm not good at getting myself up to speed. That's something I need to work on, along with most sailors. By being honest, I can estimate before an event where I'll finish within one or two places. It's a matter of knowing your own abilities.

But that prediction is easier for me because I'm not an emotional sailor. Some people have real highs and lows. One 470 skipper will put together a superb regatta and then he'll be way down in the tank at the next race. That's a matter of negative psychology; the more inconsistent you are, the less you believe that you're fast. It's also an indication of nonconservative sailing. Taking big gambles always leads to performance variations.

When I lose, I can always find some point where I didn't sail conservatively. I usually find that I took a chance someplace and it just didn't pay off. The more conservatively you sail, the better you'll do. Calculate ahead and sail to a steady plan. Consistency in results is always a sign of a steady sailor.

Most people don't realize that if you hve excellent boatspeed, you can take some chances. If you don't have speed, you have to sail cautiously. Too often, skippers do just the opposite. When they find that they are going poorly, they start taking big gambles and they invariably find themselves farther back than before.

For example, in the 1974 470 world's chmpionship, we knew after the first day of sailing that our mast was too stiff and our sails too flat for the chop we encountered. I guessed that we were about the 20th fastest boat. So we started sailing very carefully and took no chances at all. We never gambled and we ended up fourth, despite our poor boatspeed. The sixteen boats that should have been ahead of us had thrown away their advantages by making mistakes.

Any skipper who misses a skippers' meeting is just inviting trouble. Both Jack and I read the race instructions two or three times before the meeting, so we can clarify anything we don't understand at the meeting. And when both of us read the instructions, we act as safeguards to each other. If you're going to sail, you should sail well. Something as simple as the skippers' meeting or the race instructions should never be overlooked.

The main reason we arrive early is to find out about the local weather. We talk to local sailors and we go out and sail. Along with the sailing, we study weather maps. In fact, we look at the weather map in the morning, go out and sail, and then look at it when we come in to figure out what has happened. This is one area where people in the Midwest and the East have an advantage. They almost always know more about the weather because they can watch it progress across the country. West Coast sailors have no real idea of what goes on in the atmosphere. Jack and I are making a concerted effort to learn how weather affects the conditions on the race course.

On practice day, we'll even make notes of when shifts occurred, how much they were, and how often they swung. Then we try to see a relation between the morning weather prediction and what actually happened.

But the most important time is to get out at least an hour before the start and study the wind oscillations. Compare them to previous days: what happened when the winds were similar? That's why we went to Kingston every year: so we'd have a backlog of weather knowledge for the Olympic Trials nearby. We'd be able to know that on a similar day, certain things happened and we'd be able to plan ahead with some degree of accuracy. I'm not much of a reader, so our weather study is confined to the practical rather than the theoretical.

People become so used to sailing a certain way in their home waters that they cease observing what is going on about them. For example, going to the right side of most Southern California courses is the basic rule because it pays off so regularly. But if you automatically go to the right in a new area without thinking, then you're sailing stupidly. You shouldn't even have a preconceived "pattern" when sailing your home waters, but it's easy to get lulled when something works in ninety-five out of one hundred races. But in unfamiliar waters, never do it.

In an area that you aren't sure of, sail conservatively. Don't go all the way to one corner of the course unless you have a really strong reason. Sail the middle or slightly favor one side. So what if you're not first at the weather mark? I figure that if I'm in the first ten boats at the weather mark, then I'm in good shape. I'm well ahead of the pack, and I'm within easy striking distance of the leaders.

At the same time that you're searching for local knowledge, don't follow the local sailors. These are *their* home waters and they may be blind to something obvious. At CORK in 1974, we did all right in the first race by going up the middle, even though the odds say that the right side of the course is always favored. We didn't catch the significance of this and we went to the right side in the next two races, only to be 45th and 50th at the first mark. The left side was heavily favored, and I just wasn't following my own rules of always looking around.

A second problem that occurs in home waters is that everyone starts going to one side because it *seems* favored. But you never really know, because nobody goes the other way! Occasionally, somebody takes a flyer to the opposite side and has a huge lead, but it's easy to say that he was just lucky. But when you put a big fleet of boats on a course, it's obvious you've made some major mistake when you're 50th.

As a further example of the thinking you should acquire, in the two races where we were 45th and 50th at the first marks, we started sailing very, *very* cautiously. We worked at picking up by other sailor's mistakes and by sailing to, but not beyond, our capabilities. We finished second and third in those races.

I wear a wetsuit when it's cold, with sweat pants and a sweater over it. If it's warm, I'll wear shorts and a light shirt. I always were shoes to protect my feet. We both wear the French Flotherchoc life jackets because they're very light and flexible. I can't wear others because their bulk jams me under the boom on a tack. I have a bad habit though: I don't wear my life jacket unless it's required and that is foolish. I just hate life jackets.

Because you can't wear more than twenty kilograms (forty-four pounds) of wet clothing, I dress more simply. Jack also wears the wet suit with sweat clothes over to protect it. Since he's wet most of the time, he never wears foul weather gear, but I do occasionally. Basically we both dress for comfort and agility.

We never take food out on the race course. I have a good breakfast and since there's usually only one race a day, hunger is no problem. If two or three races are scheduled, then we'll take a couple of sandwiches. We always take lots of water and salt pills, even in cold conditions. You dehydrate rapidly while sailing, especially in a wetsuit, which is like a portable sauna, so you need the water and salt. Besides, we always seem to be on a diet so the food really isn't a problem.

Since your mental attitude is a part of the pre-race work, let me emphasize conservative sailing again, which is really a harp of mine. The best way to win races is by letting other people make the mistakes. Most really good sailors don't take gambles. Gambles pay off in a percentage, and you can't win them all. In fact, most major events are won by clustered scores . . . not all firsts, but several seconds, thirds, and fourths. A record like that is a sign of good conservative hard-to-beat sailing. When your results are 1–20–1–30, then you're doing something badly wrong. You should always finish within four or five boats each race.

The 1974 470 world's championship was won by a skipper who had only a single victory. I won CORK in 1974 although I won only one race. But in each case, we had a lot of seconds and thirds. Buddy Melges is fantastic at that type of sailing. He doesn't always win individual races, but he rarely drops fourth and he ends up with the silverware. By just sailing steadily and letting people around you deteriorate, you'll move steadily upwards.

When you find that there are a few sailors in your fleet who are also sailing conservatively, then you have to start turning the table and attack them. But don't take big chances.

It's hard psychologically when you've lost a few regattas to keep from gambling. You start wanting to win so badly that you forget the steady tactics that worked for you in the past. The worst time to gamble is when you're behind, and that is multiplied when you're on the first beat. You can gamble a bit on the last legs of the course, after people have spread out a little. Then you only lose a few boats at the worst. But gambling on the first leg is an all-or-nothing proposition. The boats are clustered so tightly that when you lose, you lose big. Take chances only when they can't hurt you.

At CORK in 1974, only one boat had a chance to beat us in the regatta. In the last race, we couldn't let him be in the first three places, or he'd win. We were first and second at the start, so we started sitting on his air to drive him back. It's really tough to force someone back in the fleet, but he tacked away off to one side of the course to break free of us. If he'd sailed conservatively, he probably would have been in the top three and that would have given him the regatta. After the race, he just shook his head. He knew what he'd done wrong. He had the boatspeed to stay in the top three, but the gamble hadn't paid off and he dropped to 68th place. After that, he had no chance at all.

The moral of this is: Don't be greedy, sail conservatively, and let others make the mistakes.

THE START

Chapter **7**

IF YOU'VE BEEN OUT EARLY on the course, then you've done a lot of your homework. You've studied the wind oscillations so you have a fairly good idea of the wind's pattern. You may even have made notes with a grease pencil on the deck. We do. When the race committee sets the starting line, you can see if they've set it square or angled, and, because you've timed the shifts, you'll have an idea of when the next wind oscillation can be expected. For example, a square line may become cocked if the wind swings before the start.

Races are often won or lost on your position after the first two tacks. Being able to catch the shift first, being clear of the pack . . . these can pull you into the first few boats in the fleet. The difference between the leaders and the pack is the ability to get onto the favored tack quickly, without having to duck behind a lot of boats or endure bad air.

The amount of wind oscillations often surprise people. We don't have much in the way of local shifts on the West Coast, but you can have as much as fifteen or twenty degrees in other areas. For example, CORK seems to have ten-degree oscillations on a four-minute cycle. So we had to be very aware of our time to the start because one end of the line could suddenly become very wrong. But since the Kingston shifts were so predictable, we just planned on them. What was the favored end at the preparatory signal was never the favored end at the starting gun.

I rarely try to start right at the flag. It's always too crowded. If the line is even and square to the wind, I like to start in the middle. If the line is favored toward one end, I like to start five to ten lengths down from the favored end. That keeps me clear of all the pushing and shoving at the pin, so I have good speed and clear air at the gun. If the line is really favored, then I might try for the flag end . . . simply because it is easier to get back to restart when you're over.

I go head to wind on the line to check both the wind direction and the line direction. It's so easy to eyeball that nobody should ever start at the wrong end.

We check the line at both the ten- and the five-minute guns, because the oscillations may have changed or, more likely, the flag may have dragged anchor or been moved when we didn't notice. Don't assume that anything will ever remain the same.

In the 470, Jack does all the timing: calling it out every minute down to three minutes, then every thirty seconds down to a minute, and then he counts every five seconds. We *always* have a backup watch because we've had phenomenal problems with watches. In the first race of the 1974 470 world's, we broke both watches. That's unbelievable! Jack uses a big Hever and I have a regular wrist watch, but even without our peculiar watch luck I'd still have two just in case.

At five minutes we make our decision on which end of the line is favored (or will be favored after we figure the wind shifts). But we don't stop there. We check again at two and a half minutes to make sure that we don't want to change our plans.

We always approach the start on port tack, and then we tack to starboard with about 1½ minutes to go. We try to come as close to the line as possible, leaving ourselves a little room to drift with. On port tack, you can see holes opening up much better. If you approach on the normal starboard tack, you can't make holes; they're there or not. On port, you can dive in anyplace you want and create your own hole in the line.

At one and a half minutes, everyone has pretty much solidified his position, and I want to be one of the last to make a commitment. That gives me a chance to be the leeward boat. If you sit luffing on starboard tack waiting for the gun, somebody will invariably come up below you. But if you're the last boat moving, you can always leave a hole to leeward.

I start this way in both big and small fleets, and it's been very successful. I don't like timed runs because they are too inflexible. If anything happens at all, your timing is off. That might be acceptable for ocean racers that don't speed up or slow down much, but in a dinghy, any change in the wind puts you either ahead or behind your planned time, which is an unnecessary extra problem. By port tacking, you're still going to start sheeting in to have full speed at about fifteen seconds before the gun, plus you have full control over your starting position up to and after that point.

One reason that I start in the middle, especially in big fleets, is that the line often sags back and you can gain a boatlength right at the start by getting out ahead of the sag. If the fleet bulges out, then you're still ahead of the boats that chose to start at the flag end. No matter what happens, you're in good shape. The worst that can happen is that everyone stays straight and you have an even start.

When you start, make sure that no one is driving over you; that really hurts your speed. If that does happen, a quick little luff just after the gun usually drops him back into the boat behind him, leaving you free to charge away.

I try to have a safe leeward on all boats above me and be driving over those below me. Usually, if you can see the leeward mark at the start, then the line is sagging back. From your position in the boat, it should look like everyone will be over the line early.

The port approach seems to eliminate a lot of problems—you have no one below you, you're able to pick your spot, and you're close to the line. A hole to leeward is more important than one to windward. If the boat below you can slow you up, then the boat to windward of you will go past and you're dead. But if you have that space to leeward, you can drive off with the boat above you and you won't be hurt. So always keep the leeward side open.

I see a lot of people getting within five seconds of the start, sheeting in, and then driving down into the leeward hole that they've so carefully protected. That closes the hole and automatically gives your downwind competitor a safe leeward on you. You should sheet in and leave the hole untouched. That guarantees you forty or fifty boat lengths of clear sailing even if the next boat below you is able to pinch up and hurt you eventually. Just remember that you can sail for a long way in clear air if you start ten feet above the leeward boat.

If you start at the middle of the line and there is a header, you can probably cross most of the boats above you. I'd be willing to duck ten boats to go the right way on a windshift. The bad problem is if you start at the middle and the wind lifts. Then everyone moves up on you. Many sailors tack at that point, because they don't realize it's a shift and they think the fleet is driving over them. In that situation, assuming you've been watching the compass and know that it's a lift, the best thing is to wait until the wind goes back the other way. That's why a compass can tell whether there's been a slight lift or whether you're being eaten up on boatspeed. The difference is very important for your mental health.

Analyze the first couple of shifts. Are they the type you sail into and then tack, or are they just little oscillations? If the shift appears to be permanent, then you should tack into it. If it's going to swing back, you probably ought to keep going. And the only way you can tell is by your hour of checking before the start.

If you know you're going to be early, particularly if the one-minute rule applies, try to shove everyone over with you. Try to force a recall. That's pretty easy, really . . . keep forcing boats up, especially if you're near the flag end. The 470 class has been using a DSQ rule for boats over the line in the last minute. If you're over and you think you've been spotted, you'd darn well better force a restart or you're out of the race.

In other situations, you have two choices: jam everyone else over the line to force a recall or instantly start going for an end to restart yourself. If it's the first start and the one-minute rule doesn't apply, I'd always try to force more boats over. The race committee, if there's any doubt, will almost always have a general recall and restart the first race. So if you go back, you'll really end up in the tank. After the first recall, race committees start getting tougher; they tend to throw boats out for being over rather than have another recall. At that point, get back and restart as fast as you can.

A lot of people worry about looking for the weather mark right after the start. The position of the weather mark, unless it's so far off center that you're faced with a one-tack beat, should never affect your early race decisions. At that point, you should sail to get ahead of the mob rather than head for the mark.

Sail for speed rather than position on the course right after the start. Getting to the favored side of the course by throwing away your fleet position isn't wise usually.

At the start, the main idea is to be going as fast as possible, as far forward as possible, without being seen. It sounds terrible, but it's true.

THE BEAT

Chapter **8**

ONCE YOU'VE STARTED, it's time to settle down and keep the boat moving as quickly as possible in the right direction. The predominant reason for poor boatspeed upwind is incorrect sail trim rather than poor helmsmanship.

Sail trim is basically the same in both trapeze and non-trapeze boats. The mainsail should be tightened by either the Cunningham or downhaul until the wrinkles are just barely showing along the luff. Always sail with some contraction wrinkles flowing aft . . . that keeps you from overtightening the luff. If the luff is too tightly stretched, you'll notice a fold or hard spot along the mast; if the luff is too loose, you'll have large wrinkles running aft from the mast. The same applies to the outhaul, except that you want to have the foot of the sail smooth and not wrinkled along the boom (assuming, of course, that you haven't got a loose-footed sail).

In under ten knots of wind, most small boats should have the boom almost centered—not quite, but very near. As you have to start hiking out, ease the boom down toward the rail until, when you're having to stay fully hiked out, the boom is at the rail. The theory boils down to: boats that are easy to hold down and which move easily can have the boom kept inboard longer. Heavy boats, like Snipes and Lidos, should have the boom eased earlier since they have to foot earlier.

The jib is trimmed in the same way as the mainsail. Adjust the halyard tension or, if you have it, the luff downhaul, to remove most of the luff wrinkles.

When setting the jib fairleads, we've found that it's easiest if

you imagine two marks on the leech, at the one-third and two-thirds points. When the lead is set correctly, the leech should sag off five degrees at the top mark and it should hook to weather five degrees at the bottom mark. The best explanation for this is that it closely duplicates your mainsail twist and so creates an even slot effect.

When trimming the mainsail, the top batten should be kept parallel with the boom. That keeps the sail from twisting off too much and also allows the boom to move in and out without disturbing the sail shape. (See figure.) In light air and chop, hooking the mainsail by tightening either the vang or the mainsheet gives more power, particularly when the boom is eased farther off the centerline. The tighter leach combined with footing produces the best speed in light wind conditions.

The decision whether to pinch or to foot should be a function of the conditions. A really good sailor can do either depending upon the wind and chop. Smooth water and a bunch of boats around you dictates pinching to force them back. Chop and boats around you forces you to foot to keep from stalling. You should be adaptable and not get into the habit of thinking of yourself as either a pincher or a footer.

In drifting conditions, you have two choices. Some people try to make their sails very full, but I try to flatten them out by tightening the outhaul, which decreases draft yet keeps it fairly well aft instead of moving it forward. In pure drifting conditions, I think a flat foil shape is most effective.

In survival conditions when you have too much wind, flatten the sail again, keep the boom eased, and keep your jib leads outside. Be careful, though, because it's easy to go too far and end

■ *With the jib luff breaking slightly (just forward of the window), this Lido is sailing both high and fast. The backwind in the main is acceptable, and the general boat trim is ideal for the smooth water and medium breeze.*

up reaching around the course. The most important thing in lots of wind is to pull the centerboard up to ease the weather helm. The 470 board should come up about halfway, as does the Coronado-15's. The Lido-14 seems to respond to raising it a quarter of the way. Cocking the centerboard makes the boat go faster forward, and it doesn't stall as easily.

We've also found that most boats, like the Snipe, go best when you reduce the mast rake in heavy air, but the 470 is much easier to hold down if you add extreme rake. We start letting the 470 mast aft by easing the jib halyard in about 18 knots of wind, and we start going forward on the Snipe at about twenty knots.

In normal winds, I set the centerboard vertical and in light airs I allow it to angle forward if the class rules allow it.

If you don't make all the adjustments in the 470 (which is representative of the 505 and other light planing boats), it develops so much weather helm that you almost can't sail around the course when the wind is over twenty knots. When you do make the adjustments, it planes to weather with almost a neutral helm.

Since most trapeze boats are very light, the most important thing is to keep the boat absolutely flat in a breeze. Heavy boats like the Snipe can heel over a bit, but a really fast dinghy has to be on its lines. So you should set your sails with that in mind. The traveler should be to weather to keep the boom on centerline. As the wind comes up, we sheet less hard so the mainsail twists off and we end up sailing on the bottom of the sail which has less heeling leverage.

I don't think enough people allow their sail to twist. Too many oversheet the mainsail. Remember that there is a different

■ *In drifting conditions, crew weight should be centered, the boat should be heeled slightly to leeward (so that gravity can help hold the sails full), and sail trim should be looser than normal breezes. Speed is critical, and pointing ability should be sacrificed to keep speed up.*

■ *Keeping any small boat flat is very critical when going upwind, particularly one so beamy as these Lidos. A small amount of heel angle will quickly bury a large amount of wetted area and the boat will slow down quickly. In this case, the skipper on port tack should ease his main to get the boat "on her feet" again.*

■ *Beating in light air, Ullman pulls the trapeze to weather to ease the leech of the mainsail for speed. Note that the boom end is still in the same position as it would be for more wind, but the leech has developed a pronounced curve and the top batten is well to leeward. By keeping the crew on the centerboard well, Ullman has a good view of the jib luff and still keeps the boat level.*

wind at the top of your mast because of the surface drag close to the water level. The top third of your mainsail is in a stronger wind that has changed direction aft (because of your speed through the water), so the top of the sail may be three to four degrees more toward a reach than the bottom of the sail. For that reason, twist is not the foe that it was once considered. With twist, you are just allowing the mainsail to set properly for winds both high and low.

Mast bend depends on the boat and the conditions. If you can hold the boat flat and the main doesn't have too much luff curve, then don't bend the mast. In the 470, you can almost always hold the boat down, so a straight mast is nice. The exception to this is with the Z-Spar mast in a very bad chop, where the bend helps you work through waves. The whole rig flexes easily.

In the Snipe, which is hard to hold down, we're using a very bendy spar to flatten the sail when the wind comes up. Just be sure that your mast bends down low. A mast bending up high is no good. By bending low, you're opening up the leech and flattening the bottom of the sail, which gives really good speed in a breeze. As soon as the mast bends more than the luff curve in the sail, the leech will twist and open in the top of the sail. I've never been able to understand why, but for some reason this doesn't affect the lower leech.

Going to weather in the 470, Jack concentrates on keeping the boat flat and watching the compass. Unless I ask him, he doesn't watch boats around us. I expect him to tell me if we're on a lift or a header, and he has to be ready to tell me if we're up or

■ *Punching to weather in a breeze, this FD crew is close together to minimize hobbyhorsing, and the crew has his weight (including one arm) as far outboard as possible to produce the maximum heeling force. Because the FD is overpowered, the main is completely flogging and the power is generated in a breeze by the genoa.*

down without having to stop and figure. I don't think the skipper
should have to read the compass . . . it's too much of a distrac-
tion.

You can also get into trouble by watching the other boats too
much. I sail my own boat and worry about going as fast as I can at
all times. But I still like to be able to check around a bit too, just
to monitor the fleet. As I mentioned before, sailing blindfolded
has helped to develop an ability to look around and still sail fast;
it becomes a matter of feel. That also frees your mind to think
about tactics instead of consciously sailing the boat through the
water.

All small boats should be sailed level fore-and-aft in most conditions. In the 470, we move aft a bit when the wind reaches 18
knots to get the bow out of the water and initiate planing to
weather. In light airs the Europeans move forward, but I haven't
seen it really improve their speed, so we don't. If your transom is
definitely dragging, then I'd certainly move forward but that only
indicates that your crew weight is off balance somehow.

We allow the boat to heel slightly to leeward in light airs,
which gives a bit of weather helm for sensitive feel as well as
helping to fill the sails by gravity.

In a hard-chined boat like a Snipe, you want to sail with the
weather chine just out of the water to cut the wetted surface.
Burying the leeward chine also tends to push the boat to weather
slightly, which is helpful.

Roll-tacking is absolutely essential in all non-trapeze boats, or
in trapeze boats in light air. It's nearly impossible, or at least very
hazardous, to attempt a roll tack while your crew is trapezing. A

■ *Trapezing upwind in medium air, Ullman shows the amount
of mast rake necessary to achieve both pointing ability and boat
speed. The crew is centered together and are keeping the bow
slightly out of the water. As the breeze increases, the boom would
move closer and closer to the stern deck.*

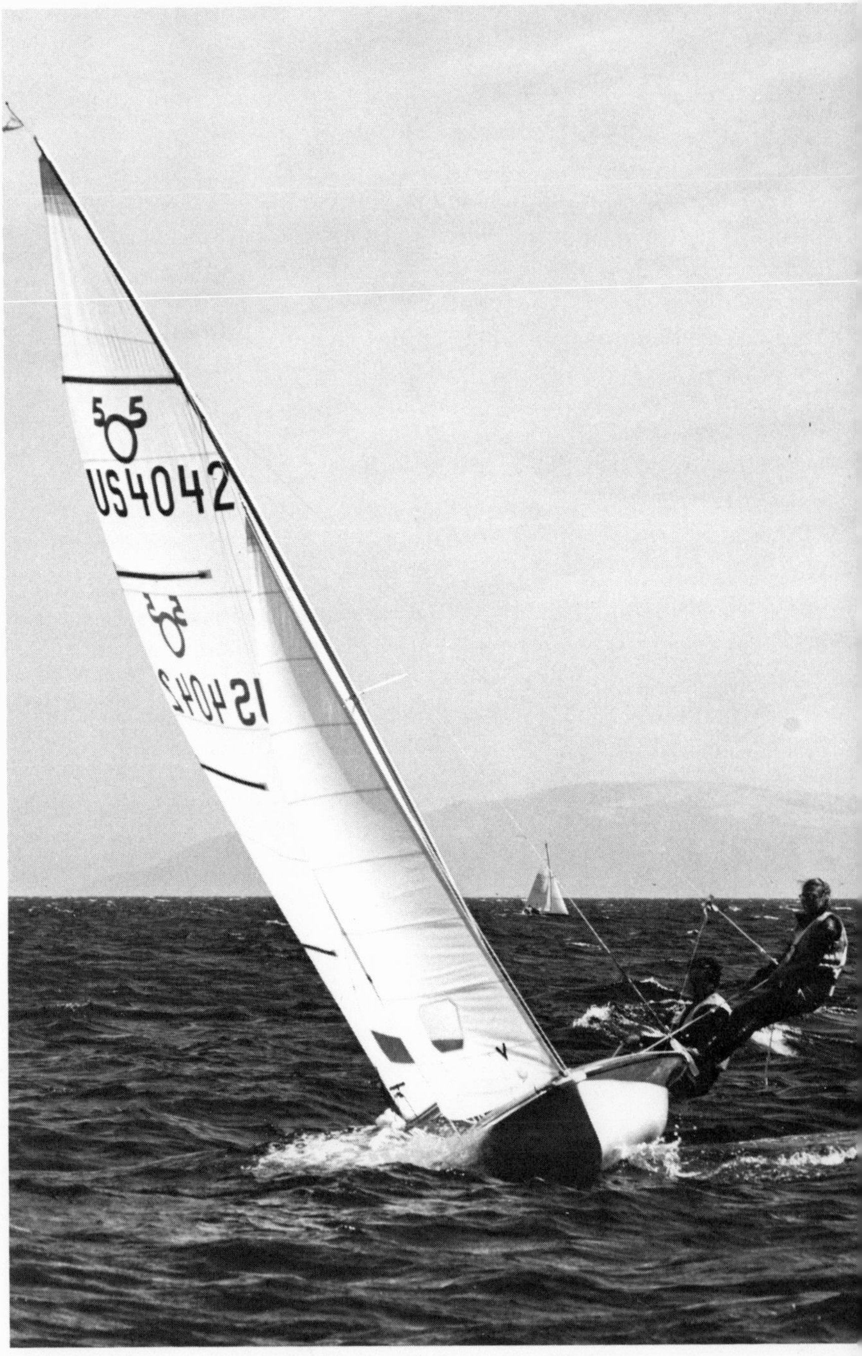
US4042

roll tack is just a way of accelerating your boat while you are tacking . . . you maintain speed and you can even gain ground to
windward by doing it. As I start my tack, I let the mainsail out
slightly and hike out to windward. What we're doing is rapidly
heeling the boat to weather as we tack. This roll holds the sails
full instead of allowing them to luff as in a conventional tack. As
the boat passes through head to wind, the jib backs and both of
us cross the boat quickly. The jib is snapped in hard on the opposite tack by the crew, and I snap the main in . . . both maneu-
vers again intended to fill the sails before they might fill otherwise. You also hike hard to bring the boat upright, which adds
even more acceleration. On this last effort to level the boat
quickly, your centerboard digs into the water as the boat comes
upright, which pulls you up to windward neatly.

A well-executed roll tack gains about half a boat length to
windward and three-fourths of a length ahead (of a conventional
tack). Multiply that by the number of tacks you make in a race,
and you can see the advantage of roll tacks.

Remember to use the helm gently in the roll tack. All the
snapping and jerking should be done on the hull itself and you
don't want to stall the rudder. We heel the boat as much as we
can without capsizing in the initial roll. The more you do and the
harder you do it, the more you will gain. With the exception of
the rudder movement, the roll tack is not a subtle motion at all.

After the start, my basic tactic is to try to stay clear of groups
of boats. They tend to slow each other down progressively, and
they disturb the wind around them.

I make an effort to sail the first two wind shifts as well as pos-

■ *By hunching forward into a "sitting" position, this crew is
robbing the 505 of valuable weight to counteract the heeling forces.
Keeping the crew "out flat" is vitally important in heavy air. Both
main and jib are eased a bit too much for good upwind performance, and the jib luff should be much tighter also.*

sible, even to the extent of ducking boats to stay within my plan. Before the start, I have an idea of what side of the course is preferred, and I try to sail the "middle" of that side for the first fourth of the leg. At that point, I'll look around and decide if I want to go deeper to that side. If the wind is oscillating a lot, I'll tend to stay in the middle for safety. If it's steady, I'll commit to go farther on the good side because the chances of a big shift and the resultant big loss are less.

If someone persists in sitting on your wind, it's usually fairly easy to sail him under someone else, which encourages him to lose interest in you for his own sake. People using their heads will keep a loose cover on a fast boat if they want to see where you're going or if they just want to stay near. Unless you're on the last leg of the course, a tight cover is just asking for trouble.

My primary goal in the first four minutes after the start is to get my wind free and my boatspeed up. Then I start thinking about going the right direction. If you reverse those ideas, you'll end up behind the fleet.

I like the port tack approach as I near the weather mark, particularly if I'm in a crowd of boats, for the same reasons that I port tack the start. The starboard tack layline is a terrible place to be unless you're all alone: there are boats above you unless you've overstood badly, and there are always boats coming in and tacking on your lee bow.

I have a definite aversion to being on any layline for any distance; you just never win. Once you reach the layline, you have removed your option to play shifts. The layline is also a bad choice on the percentages. Your only hope is for the wind to remain constant. If you get a header when you're on the layline, then the boats to leeward of you in the middle of the course will either gain or pass you. If you get a lift, then you've overstood and the boats to leeward will gain again. And unless you're first, you have to struggle through wind and water that has just been occupied by someone else. Avoid laylines like the plague.

You'll find that the left side of the course near the windward mark is always less crowded, because everyone has a mind set about approaching the mark on starboard. With less of a crowd, the wind is always better, so you can gain a lot of ground on the starboard tack boats.

To summarize my ideas on the beats: sail alone as much as possible; play the shifts to the best of your ability; and stay away from laylines on either side of the course. When you decide to gamble, don't do it on the first beat because you'll lose places since everyone is bunched up. Gamble on the later beats, where you'll only lose distance and not numbers.

Sail the boat differently for each type of wind and sea condition, but keep it flat and moving at all times.

THE REACH

Chapter **9**

ASSUMING A TYPICAL COURSE, you have some decisions to make as you reach the weather mark. You should probably start reviewing the options available to you before you reach the mark, so that you can take advantage of situations as they arise.

When you have the opportunity, you should sail either straight for the jibe mark or slightly below it. Sailing high only adds distance to your race . . . which other boats may not add to theirs. By sailing above the rhumb line course to the next mark, you give yourself an illusion of going faster, which is probably true. Any boat goes faster if you reach up. But when you get to the end of the reach, the rule of "what goes up must come down" applies and you'll slow considerably as you head back down to the mark from your high course.

By the same token, if you round the weather mark by yourself, you might sail slightly below the next mark to give yourself the opportunity of reaching up fast at the end of the leg and picking off boats right at the mark.

If you are in the midst of a large cluster of boats, then you'll have to take different action to get ahead. Probably the best option is to drive ten or fifteen degrees high right at first; get above them so you have a chance to drive over them later. Your disturbed air won't do them any good, and you'll be free to sail your own course.

If you're behind a big cluster of boats, consider diving below them on the reach. Groups of boats have a tendency to keep going higher and higher above course in a defensive attempt to keep boats from going above them, which leads everyone far off

■ *This photo shows several important points about reaching in heavy weather. The crew has adjusted his trapeze height so that he remains free of the water and bow wave, yet he is still effectively outboard. Both skipper and crew have moved aft slightly to help maintain the plane. The extremely tight vang is maintaining the sail shape while the mainsheet is primarily for lateral control.*

course. If you can nip below them at the beginning of the reach, they'll soon be far above you and you won't be in their bad air. Besides, you'll be ahead of them at the next mark because they'll be going very slowly at the end of the reach.

We usually set our spinnaker pole early in light airs, and then pop the chute up as soon as we turn the mark. If the wind is stronger and we're in planing conditions, then we do everything after we round the mark. In fact, we've been very successful in some cases by delaying our spinnaker set. You always slow down slightly while you're struggling with the spinnaker set and, if you're just behind a group of boats that are busy with their spinnakers, you can sail high over their wind and then set your own spinnaker. In that way, you're slowing them down with your bad air at the same time that you slow down with the set. The end effect is that you are above them and ready to drive over them quickly.

If there is no tactical situation that prevents it, try to work the boat downwind as much as possible on the reaches. A tactical situation would be a boat very close that you don't want to pass you, or a boat just below you. But barring these instances, it's best to work continually at sailing low of your course. It always seems that you end up right on the mark if you do. It's very strange how you tend to sail high on reaches . . . the waves and your weather helm are always working you upwind. So you should constantly think about working down: drive off in the puffs; drive off on waves.

If you find someone behind you with better boatspeed, don't try to tangle with him at all. Just let him by as easily as possible by driving off. If you start luffing each other, you'll go far off course, he'll pass you anyway because he has better speed, and

■ *A hard-driven Flying Dutchman broad-reaching in heavy wind. Both skipper and crew are well-aft, the main is eased far out, and the boat is sailing primarily on the genoa. Note the comfortable attitude of the crew, who is well above the waterlevel.*

you'll lose other boats that you should have beaten.

With a non-spinnaker boat, everyone puts the pole up too early. It's a follow-the-leader situation. The first boat sets his whisker pole and then everyone automatically follows suit. You'll find that you can use your jib effectively quite a way downwind—that is, with the wind well abaft the beam. To keep it full takes the full attention of both crew and skipper, but you'll find that it's really fast.

On a course that is just marginal for setting either a spinnaker or a whisker pole, you'll find that courses tend to diverge. Those who have chosen to set poles or chutes will drop off downwind. Those continuing with jibs will head up. If you can sail the middle course directly for the mark, you'll always come out a hero. It's very hard to work a boat downwind if you aren't using your whisker pole or spinnaker, but it's very important. You have to slide off on every wave and think to yourself; down, down, down. It's easy to sail high and look like you're going fast, but when you get to the mark, you're dead.

If you take the time to practice reaching without chute or pole, you'll soon pick up the technique. The whisker pole or chute limits you tactically, since you can't respond easily to a luff. You're really only able to go down. If you aren't using the pole, you can go up easily.

I rock the boat and pump the mainsail to help slide off as much as possible on each wave. Drive down in every puff of wind (it helps keep your sails full), and sail higher on the lulls to keep your boatspeed up. Just as you catch a wave, rock the boat to weather and pump the main in. That little acceleration (just like in a roll tack) can squirt you onto the face of a wave that you might otherwise miss. Assume that you can gain five feet on each wave . . . consider what catching ten or fifteen waves that other boats miss will do for your finish position! In a chine boat like a Snipe, the weather chine buries in the water and helps to shove you to leeward. It's just the reverse of burying the lee chine when going to weather.

In planing conditions in a non-spinnaker boat, you work harder to stay on a plane; you have to rock and pump and catch every wave. In a spinnaker boat, you pretty much follow the chute and try to keep going at maximum speed. I hardly ever pump the 470. I try to keep the chute full and follow it through the waves and still work down without disturbing the plane. The 470 catches waves without too much effort because it's so light. But don't lose sight of your objective: getting to the next mark fast. Sailors sometimes get involved in surfing on waves and wander off course. Even though they're going fast, they'll lose places. Sometimes it's just tactically smart to get *off* a wave.

There's a whole rule section on pumping that every sailor should read, because you do as much as they allow, plus just a touch. You see big gains because of rocking and pumping, and you don't ever see winners that don't rock or pump. In the end, I'm sure we'll have rocking allowed . . . it'll be a part of accepted sailing technique. I don't know about pumping, but it's pretty hard to determine what's legal and what isn't. Years ago, roll tacks were considered unethical and now they're an integral part of racing. These methods are merely techniques, nothing more or less.

The jib should be completely barber-hauled outboard on reaches. That brings up a point about barberhaulers. Too many boats put the barberhauler directly outboard of the normal jib lead. The barberhauler should be placed on or forward of a radius drawn from the jib tack. As you reach off and ease the jib, you need to tighten the leech of the jib, and the only way you can do that is to move the lead (or barberhauler) forward.

The jib should be made as full as possible by easing either the downhaul or the halyard tension, and it should be let out as far as possible. Nothing slows a boat as much as an overtrimmed jib. When the jib is too tight, it makes the mainsail look loose, and you end up with both sails overtrimmed, which results in zero boatspeed. The crew should always play the jib on reaches . . . don't ever expect to win with a cleated jibsheet. As you play the

■ *This FD crew is trapezing improperly and could lead to a capsize. His height is too close to the water, and a slight drop in wind strength could cause him to drag in the water or be swept off his feet. When reaching, the crew should be higher so that they could swing inboard quickly without hitting the gunwale.*

boat in the puffs or on waves, the crew should be keeping the jib full.

The main should have the outhaul and Cunningham or down-haul released, the vang should be tight enough to keep the top batten parallel with the boom or, in planing conditions, slightly tighter. The mast should be held in its aft position on loose rigged boats, and it should be as straight as possible. At the same time, the headstay should be tight. Some people allow the headstay and the jib luff to sag, but that makes the jib much harder to trim, and it also allows the whole rig to flop around, which disturbs the flow of wind over the sails. With a loose rig, the boat is probably marginally faster on a reach if the mast is plumb vertical, but the loose headstay negates any advantage, so I recommend sailing with aft mast rake on reaches.

Keep the sails out as far as they'll go without luffing. I don't particularly like yarns on sail, and I think the best indication of correct sail trim is the occasional luff.

The centerboard should be up just enough so that you have a slight weather helm. In the 470, that's about one-third of the way up because the added area of the spinnaker helps to balance the helm. In a non-spinnaker boat like the Lido or Coronado, you'll have to bring the board at least halfway up.

When you have planing breezes, move aft a little bit so that the boat is in a planing attitude. That way the bow doesn't either dip or rise when it starts onto a plane, so you get onto the plane with a minimum expenditure of energy. The boat just sails onto it without struggling.

I think you should move forward a bit in light airs on the reach, but don't overdo it. In Lidos, I see people practically sitting on the foredeck, which is ridiculous. They are submerging the very fat mid and fore sections of the hull, which is a lot more drag than having the transom in the water.

In survival conditions, you'll sail mostly on either the jib or the chute while reaching. Don't worry too much about the main; it can just flog until the wind eases and you can trim some of it in. A technique that few people use is to let the boom vang off a bit. With vang tight, once the boom hits the water it can't be eased any further and you'll probably capsize. The loose vang allows it to lift and skip on the water.

In heavy air, your problem is not going to be catching waves, but negotiating the next wave. You're going to be traveling at much more than the speed of the wave, so you'll pass each one quickly. The trick is to be able to get up the face of the next wave as cleanly as possible. On a reach, unless the waves are not from the direction of the wind, you'll have to feather up slightly as you reach the bottom of the trough so you don't just jam the bow into the wave. As you go over the crest of each wave, you have a chance to drive off slightly to keep working down, but be prepared to come up as you reach the next trough. The whole S-course takes practice and is a new problem to work on. Just remember that the two places where you're likely to stop or stall are at the very top and the very bottom of each wave set.

A critical area on the reaching leg isn't even on the leg: it's on the approach to the weather mark. If there is a boat above you, the chances are excellent that he'll drive over you as you reach off. You could drive off very low to get clear air, but he'll probably nail you anyway. So the best plan is to drop him back with a quick luff before you get to the mark. If you can, always set yourself up to be clear as you round the mark because once you've rounded, you're committed to that position for the reach. I've heard people say that a luff at the mark is either illegal or unsportsmanlike, but often these are the same people who will slam a quick luff into you as you reach past them to windward. I'm convinced that giving yourself a clear area as you round the weather mark is just as important as opening a hole to leeward at the start.

As you approach the jibe mark, you should be a bit low so that you have plenty of boatspeed to either break or establish an overlap. As we round, we jibe the mainsail first or, rather, I take the spinnaker sheets and Jack shoves the main across. Then he stands up and jibes the pole and we're off again. Whoever handles the spinnaker sheets has to be sure that the spinnaker is moved completely around the headstay so that, after the jibe, the chute doesn't fold back over the headstay as the boat accelerates. In a non-spinnaker boat, my crew still jibes the main across for me, usually by grabbing the vang and yanking it across. That's much faster than my trying to hand-over-hand the mainsheet.

Just after we jibe, I sail at least twenty degrees above course just to be sure nobody sails inside me. This shuts the door on those people very firmly. If one boat sails over you, a line will form and boats will just keep passing you as you get slower and slower. This also clears us from anybody just below us who might feel like luffing us suddenly while we're too busy to notice. If you jibe normally and another boat drives across your stern, you've got nobody to blame but yourself.

There's also no reason to end up on the outside of a lot of boats at the mark. That happens because you weren't thinking before you got to the mark. The only exception is if you're overtaking from behind and you just haven't any place to go. But if you're ahead, you certainly ought to be the inside boat with full rights. You'll find that the confusion and mayhem progress outward from the inside boat: everyone has to give way, and they're sailing in confused water and wind. The inside boat always has clear air and you can gain an immense amount by just taking the inside path early.

If you do end up outside for some reason, just kill some time and then head us across everyone's stern. Every boat will have an overlap on the others, so they won't be able to luff to prevent your drive across behind them. The only boat that can stop you is the inside boat, but he's probably already moved away in front of the pack.

As you retrim the spinnaker for the next reach, never sheet in before the spinnaker is at the end of the pole. Otherwise you'll have a big bag off to the side that just pulls you over, not forward. We capsized at a 470 world's championship after a jibe because we sheeted too early on a tight reach. The spinnaker was only a couple of feet from the pole, but over we went. That's also a good example of non-conservative sailing. We'd been in a good position, but we dropped back to 73rd place, and that may have cost us second place. When you're behind, you just can't afford to make mistakes, so you should sail more cautiously.

A lot of people worry about the traveler position on reaches, but I don't move it at all. I depend on the vang to hold the boom down, and I trim the sail with the sheet, not the traveler. The only real use I find for the traveler is to center the boom upwind.

To summarize reaching, you should try to establish a clear space for yourself before the weather mark, sail as straight a course to the next mark as possible, stay clear of other boats, and work your sails and the waves for everything.

THE RUN

Chapter **10**

RUNNING demands the same sort of pre-mark thinking that the reaches require. Few races are won by someone who is the unquestioning follower of the lead boats. So start considering the boats around you, the wind direction, and the course to the next mark before you make the rounding.

If you have boats around you, try to clear away from them just as you did before the reaches. If the wind has changed direction, you may want to jibe immediately before you set the whiskerpole or spinnaker. Races have been lost by the blind assumption that the leeward mark is dead downwind from the weather mark. A good project for your crew is to look for the next mark so you can make a good decision on your next course.

Set your chute as quickly as you can after you've rounded; it'll add considerably to your speed going dead downwind. The spinnaker pole should always be kept at right angles to the wind, and the spinnaker sheet should be played just like a jibsheet to keep the windward leech of the chute on the edge of curling. We're putting yarn telltales on each spinnaker leech about one-third of the way up and about eight inches in from the edge. They work really well to alert you to a collapse. Use them as you would yarn on the jib, and keep them both streaming toward the center of the sail. If you have the sheet overtrimmed, the outside yarn will stall and curl backwards. We find them to be really useful when you get disoreinted while playing the spinnaker. There are times when the sail just doesn't act right and you don't know why. The yarns cure the problem.

The mainsail should be let out all the way to the shroud, and

■ *In light airs, Dave Ullman sits to leeward to permit his crew to trapeze for a better view of the spinnaker behind the jib.*

the centerboard should be completely up. The only time you need any board down is in a strong breeze when a little of the tip showing helps your steering.

On the run, I heel all dinghies to weather ten or fifteen degrees. That helps to get the sail higher and into stronger winds, it makes the boat drive off in puffs rather than round up, and it reduces wetted surface. Heeling the boat to windward also creates either neutral or a little lee helm, which is fine because the boat slides to leeward (the direction you want to go) rather than up.

The mast should be as far forward as possible, except in the Snipe, where we don't let it all the way plumb so the shrouds stay slightly loose. Take every opportunity to work down on every puff or wave. Big waves take a lot of sheet pumping to catch, while smooth water doesn't require any pumping at all.

Just assume that, if the mark is dead downwind, you'll end up jibing to get to it. The old problem of heading up rather than down is more noticeable on a run than anywhere else. A mark that you should be able to sail directly at on a run always seems to get farther off to your lee side. So every foot you gain by working to leeward is an advantage.

In light air, you have to maintain your speed and reach up. But in other conditions, you have to figure out if reaching will pay. Most sailors think that it's hard to tell, but it's not. If another boat is reaching up more, ask yourself if he's gaining on an imaginary right angle drawn from your boat's beam. If he is, then he's gaining on you. In that case, you'd better reach up more, because he's going faster toward the mark than you. The right angle theory works because he'll make the same speed when he jibes to come back to the mark, and he'll gain on that course too. This works only when you are on a dead run.

I tend not to tack downwind to either side of the course. I think it's vastly overrated. It's also like going to weather, because you're getting off to one side of the course, which is a gamble. Most people don't play the shifts when they're running, but a shift is more valuable on a run than anywhere. You should jibe on every one so that you're not going dead downwind yet you're always headed for the mark. That gives you both the fastest and the shortest course. Jack calls our shifts by watching the compass, since I always try to sail straight downwind. When we get to ten degrees off the course for the mark, we jibe. That's about the same amount of shift that we would tack on while going to weather. When you reach off to one side of the course, you can't play those shifts and your potential losses are again greater.

When I'm catching someone on the run, I sail right up to his stern, drive off to leeward, and then jibe. That's a good tactic because you're taking his wind up until you jibe, and after the jibe you're to weather of him. If he tries to jibe with you, he'll be to leeward in your bad air. Your other alternative, passing to weather, is never any good if you're close because he'll always luff you up.

When you get a slight lift while going downwind in a group of boats, if it's not enough to jibe on you should sail with it as much as you can. In that way, when the wind swings back and heads you, you'll have moved forward and to weather of the other boats.

Many sailors forget that the wind *astern* of a large group of boats starts rising to pass over them, so there is always a sort of reverse wind shadow. For that reason, try to choose a course that will take you well around a clump of boats ahead on the dead run.

People also tend to relax more on runs, which is completely wrong. Increases in speed on a run are more critical than increases in speed on a beat. It is also much easier to sail fast on the beat than it is on the run. For that reason, don't let the pressure off on the run, regardless of how sunny and comfortable it is. Don't open the beer and let your mind wander. Work even harder, and you'll find that you're picking up places steadily.

On a non-spinnaker boat, the whisker pole is an absolute necessity. It should be set so that a line drawn from the tack to

■ *This side view shows the well set mainsail with a slight leech curve, the loose headstay (that allows the jib to curl free of the mainsail wind shadow), and the whiskerpole set for a dead run. Pulling the jib tight would only slow the boat down. This Lido is also heeled slightly to weather to minimize the helm.*

■ *Practice, particularly in all wind conditions, is absolutely necessary to reach the front of any class. In this case, one 470 crew is able to smoothly jibe the spinnaker while another crew winds up swimming, and it's not hard to guess which had more practices.*

the clew of the jib is at right angles to the wind. That gives you the maximum projected area as well as keeping the wind flowing across the sail and not stagnating.

If you can, plan your tactics downwind so that you will arrive at the leeward mark as the inside boat on starboard tack. That gives you a double advantage: you have the right of way outside the two-boat-length circle because you're on starboard, and you have the right of way within it since you're the inside boat. To douse our spinnaker, Jack takes the pole and I fly the spinnaker with the sheets. As soon as he removes the pole from the mast and stows it in the bilge, he pulls the chute down and stuffs it into a bag.

With any practice at all, you should be able to douse within two boat lengths of the mark. We tighten the outhaul well before that point by throwing the lever on, and we set the Cunningham once we're around the mark.

With a non-spinnaker boat, if you have to jibe to round the mark, leave the pole up until after the jibe. If you have to take the pole down first, you'll probably slow down too early. If you don't have to jibe on the rounding, then get the pole down early because you'll be reaching up for the mark.

Also be sure you round wide initially and then tighten it up so that as your stern passes the mark, you are solidly close-hauled and there is no space for anyone to duck inside you. That gives you the chance to tack early if you want to, and it also gives everyone astern of you bad air. I would even slow down a bit before the mark to let an inside boat get clear ahead if I thought I could swing inside his stern and be slightly to weather on the beat. Then I'd have him pinned down so he can't tack, and I'm ahead of him quickly.

Much of the same principles apply on the run as on the reach: sail low as much as possible, work the boat very hard, and stay clear of big clumps of boats.

The Aftermath

THIS BOOK WAS WRITTEN over a period of about one year while Dave Ullman worked and trained for the Olympics. In fact, one of the deadlines that Dave and Chris worked against was the date when Dave and his crew would leave for the Olympic Trials. Ullman had devoted a great deal of time and effort toward being the fastest 470 sailor in the United States . . . and then he wound up third at the Trials. To find out the reasons, and to see how he reacted to the non-victory, Chris and Dave got together several months after the Trials. The following interview serves as a good final chapter for this book.

NOW THAT THE SMOKE HAS CLEARED AWAY AND YOU'VE HAD A CHANCE TO RELAX AFTER THE TRIALS, WHAT ARE YOUR PLANS?

Well, I'm going to try again next time, but I plan to do it much differently. I'm going to intensify my training so that the whole program won't last as long, and I'm going to race more and practice less.

WHAT WAS THE PROBLEM WITH YOUR EFFORT IN 1976?

We simply sailed too much and we didn't race enough. When we finally got to the Trials, the racing situation felt a little foreign. We'd done too much side-by-side practicing and we'd concentrated too much on boatspeed. Speed is great, but we'd sailed in only a handful of actual regattas that year, which just wasn't enough.

At the Trials, our starting technique was off just a bit, our tac-

tics weren't as good as they'd been a year before, and our antici-
pation of situations was slow. It was all my fault, though. We'd
gone to Europe to race, but we should have stayed for a couple of
months to test ourselves in 10 or 15 regattas.

*HOW WILL YOU CHANGE YOUR "GAME PLAN" FOR
THE NEXT OLYMPICS?*

I'll shorten the period of training and just race as much as we
can. In 1980, everything important in the 470 class will be in
Europe so we'll probably spend the winter there to race. Because
the Olympics are over there, the Europeans won't come to North
America to race so I'll have to be there to train against the really
top caliber sailors. But more time in Europe means more ex-
penses next time. Our costs this time weren't too bad if you don't
count the thousands and thousands of hours we put in.

HOW MUCH TIME WILL YOU SPEND NEXT TIME?

I think about a year and a half to push hard. Between now
and then, I'm going to sail in some other classes. I plan to build a
Quarter Tonner, sail 470s and 505s, plus Snipes, Lidos, and
Thistles. But I'll take it year by year and see what regattas are ac-
cessible.

*DO YOU FEEL BADLY ABOUT PLACING THIRD IN THE
TRIALS?*

No. Well, yes, I feel bad that we placed third, but the whole
thing was an excellent learning process. I gained a tremendous
insight into all kinds of things: myself, people in general, what it
takes to win, and what it takes to make a boat go fast. They all
apply to life and not just to sailboat racing, so it was a worthwhile
experience.

You know, I think it's good every once in a while to really
dedicate yourself to something and work at it very, very hard; to
really throw yourself into something. But you can't do it too
often. In sailing, you can't do this with a National Championship
because it comes along every year. But the Olympics come every
four years, so that alone makes you work harder for the Gold
Medal.

But few people are willing to make this full commitment, and only a few in the United States really worked at the last Olympics. Out of the six that sailed, several had made that all-out effort, so it does pay off.

WHY DO YOU TRY SO HARD FOR THE OLYMPICS IF THE PRESSURE IS SO HIGH? FOR BUSINESS?

Not for business. In fact, it would be better for business not to even look at the Olympics or the Olympic classes. It's bad for business because the time input versus the dollar output just isn't there.

THEN WHY?

To be truthful, it's the glory. The Olympics have been so blown up by the media that it's the ultimate in recognition. Maybe not in sailing ability, but it's still a damn good test of skill. It's a one-shot, do-or-die week but, because of the build-up, it's still a dream.

For me, the Pan-American Games were just a taste. First, you walk into a stadium with 180,000 people screaming and yelling. Then you go up and they place a medal around your neck while they play your national anthem. You'll hear it from anybody who's won a medal and it sounds corny, but it is an unbelievable thrill. You know, I cried, and I never cry.

And I'll be back in 1980 trying just as hard for that Gold Medal.

Appendix

International 470

Idiosyncrasies / The 470 is light and quick, and it does things very fast. It's always short on power because it has so little sail area, which is opposite to most boats, so you have to realize that you can (and must) use all the available sail area that you have. But it's not a tricky boat and, in fact, I'd say it's quite forgiving.

Boat Types / The class is very strictly controlled, and most 470s seem to be comparable in speed. Some are a little better built than others, and the Vanguard and Parker hulls seem to be the strongest right now. But there really is little difference in actual boatspeed.

Crew Size / There are two weights for the combined skipper and crew in this class: the optimum weight, and what you can get away with. The best weight is between 265 and 275 pounds, with the biggest crew and the smallest skipper you can have. The parameters of still being competitive range from about 250 pounds to about 320. Some of the Europeans, and one East German crew in particular, are very fast at well over 300 pounds. They're very fast in a breeze but, of course, they aren't so great in light air. Yet they still finished in the top ten of the 1975 World Championships, so the 470 doesn't require as narrow a weight range as some people think.

Mast Rake / A tape measure run from the main halyard (in locked position) to the highest point on the transom is the best way to check mast rake in this class.

With both the Elvstrom and the Z-Spar, we use 22-feet 1-inch for normal or medium airs (5 to 15 knots), 22-feet 3-inches for light airs, and 21-feet 11-inches for over 15 knots of wind.

We leave our spar in the middle range most of the time and change it only if we're very sure that the wind will be either very strong or very light.

The mast step is halfway aft in the legal range with the Z-Spar, and all the way forward with the Elvstrom because of the differences in bend.

Mast Control / We use a wire around the front of the spar at the partners to restrict mast bend, and our spreaders are in line with the shrouds without any loading in any direction. With the Z-Spar, we use two to three inches of bend in the mast at all times, but we use no bend at all with the Elvstrom mast. We're using the Z-Spar exclusively now because it seems to be much faster, but the Elvstrom is still better in light airs and smooth water.

Shroud Tension / Very, very tight. In fact, as tight as you can get it without deforming the boat itself. I have a 16-to-1 block and tackle on the jib halyard to control it, but a powerbox would also be fine.

Jib Lead / We don't have barber haulers at all in normal conditions. We can rig them if it blows very hard, but I wouldn't recommend using them in normal conditions. There's nothing special about leading the jib otherwise; just get it so that it sets well.

Centerboard / The pivot pin should be all the way aft in the tolerances. You want to angle the board forward in light airs, and this is the only way you can do it without having it hit the front of the well too soon. With the pivot pin all the way aft, you can get about ten degrees of forward angle.

In strong breezes, we pull the board up about one-fourth with the Elvstrom mast to balance the boat, but we don't change the board with the Z-Spar.

Traveler / With the Z-Spar, we keep the traveler to weather two to three inches in 10 to 12 knots of wind with the boom vang slack. To control the leech, we sheet the main hard. At 12 knots and above, I start using the vang to hold the boom down and I pull the traveler all the way to windward. Then I use the mainsheet only to move the boom in and out, not up or down, so leech control is a function of the vang. With the Z-Spar, your boom will always be off centerline, from a couple of inches in light air to over the corner of the transom in heavy. That's because the mast tip bends sideways considerably. The Elvstrom spar is much better for beginners, because it does everything for you, and you can keep your boom amidships longer.

Crew Placement / In all but very heavy wind, the crew should stand quite far forward—just aft of the chainplate, in fact. That gets the knuckle of the bow into the water and it stops pounding. As soon as you can plane, move the crew aft. With the crew forward, you don't have to huddle too close together because the 470 doesn't seem to hobbyhorse with the weight separated.

Boat Trim / Keep the 470 flat at all times that the crew is trapezing, and let it heel slightly to leeward in lighter air to increase the feel of the rudder. That's pretty true for most trapeze boats, but a lot of skippers let the boat heel even in a breeze. That just slows you down.

Sheeting / When you aren't on the trapeze, you should sheet the jib and the main fairly hard. As soon as there is enough wind to trapeze, you can ease the jib slightly and let the leech of the mainsail twist a bit by easing the mainsheet to keep the boat moving fast.

Lido-14

Idiosyncrasies / The Lido is amazing because you pinch it constantly to go upwind. Go as high as you can at all times and never, never try to drive. It just doesn't work. The hardest conversion for me is to go from a 470 to a Lido, because it takes a while to get on the wind in the Lido. I'll sail along to windward of someone and decide to drive over him as I might in a 470. When I ease off a bit, all that happens is that I sink down into him! The Lido doesn't go any faster when sailed very full.

In smooth water, sail with the jib just feathering at all times so that you know you're on the verge of luffing. In chop, sail with the jib on the edge but not quite luffing. Just remember never to drive off. That's why I like Lidos, though: it's all tactics. You can't grind another boat down with pure boatspeed; you have to outthink him, which is one thing to say for low-performance boats.

Boat Types / They're all built by the same manufacturer, so there are no options here. Just be sure that you're close to the minimum hull weight of 310 pounds. If a boat were above or below that weight by more than 10 pounds, I'd reject it.

Crew Size / The minimum weight is 300 pounds, so stay as close to that as you can. If possible, weigh under the minimum and then carry lead to be legal. You can put the lead low in the boat and it will be more useful than having a heavy crew, who doesn't help much except in very heavy winds.

Mast Rake / With the halyard fully hoisted, measure from the shackle to the transom. For the new sailor, I think 20 feet, 8½ inches with the shrouds fairly tight is a good starting point. I use a loose rig with 20 feet, 4 inches with the mast pulled aft and 20 feet, 11 inches with it pushed forward. The loose rig is faster, but it requires constant retrimming of the sails as the spar moves around. In a lot of wind, I'll limit my aft rake to 20 feet, 6 inches to help balance the boat, and even then I'll have to pull the centerboard up a bit.

Jib Lead / Since the track is fixed in place, we keep our leads all the way forward in most conditions, and we could actually sheet a few inches further forward if that were permitted. When there is a lot of wind, move the lead to the middle of the track to ease off the top of the sail.

Centerboard / Make sure that the pivot assembly is as far aft as legal, which is 95 inches from the rudder. That way, you can get the board almost straight down under class rules, and the boat will pinch better.

One-quarter inch of jibe is permitted, and you need to use all of it to be competitive. Older boats had wooden centerboards that had a terrible shape, and you should have an airfoil shaped glass board for serious racing. In heavy air, I pull the centerboard up about two inches (measured by the centerboard arm) for better balance.

Traveler / It's so short on the Lido that it isn't worth doing much changing while underway. I leave mine pinned in the middle of the track until I can't hold the boat down, and then I just let it all the way out. But don't bother trying to change it all the time.

Vang / Use the vang only to keep the top batten parallel with the boom as mentioned before, and be sure to ease it off in heavy wind to let the mainsail twist so you won't be overpowered.

Crew Placement / Keep your weight together to minimize hobbyhorsing, and also to make your hiking weight more effective. Upwind, we sit right by the centerboard support and we move a little bit forward downwind.

Boat Trim / Keep the boat flat when you're hiking on the rail, let it heel a little bit when you're inside the boat on the wind. Heel the boat as far as you can to windward when running. The

Figure 18 ■

more you heel the Lido, the faster it goes downwind. Just don't capsize.

I wouldn't bother moving too far forward when running, because you'll just submerge the very full bow section.

Sheeting / Don't strap the Lido too hard, because it stalls easily. Keep the sails a little bit soft, and don't hoist the jib too tightly. You can almost have scallops in the jib luff before it's too loose. The range in the outhaul tension should be between 9 and 12 inches: 9 in heavy winds and 12 in light.

Don't use the whisker pole if you have any doubts about its effectiveness: you can fly the jib more efficiently without it at almost all times except on a dead run. Don't ever try to reach with the whisker pole because it just isn't long enough.

Miscellaneous / When you get the boat, be sure to add centerboard trunk braces to stiffen up the centerboard (see Figure 18). Without braces, the board will bend too much.

Hiking straps were an afterthought in the Lido, so be sure that you have separate straps for skipper and crew. If you try to use just one long strap, it doesn't offer enough security.

Snipe

Idiosyncrasies / The Snipe, like the Lido, is a "pincher." It doesn't go through chop well, though, because it's rather full forward. Going to weather, you should let the boat heel far enough to lift the weather chine out of the water, which cuts the drag of wetted surface and also lets the curved leeward chine force the boat to windward.

The Snipe is easier to stall than many boats, which means you can't look around very much the way you can in a 470. You have to concentrate at all times.

Boat Types / There are a number of good Snipes being built in the U.S. right now: Cyclone, Chubasco, Eichenlaub, Phoenix, and it varies among them for the fastest boat at any time. All are self-rescuing with the double bottom that is now required by class rules on new boats. The minimum weight is 385 pounds, and there is absolutely no reason for any Snipe to weigh more than that.

Crew Size / I think 290 to 310 pounds is a good combined weight for a Snipe, and this class offers an advantage to the bigger skipper who can work the boat and pump it more than the crew. It's one of the few boats where you can be competitive with a small crew.

Mast Rake / There are variables here because of the different centerboards available for the Snipe, and also the different masts.

With the Cobra mast and the small centerboard (six-inch bottom and straight front), I suggest a 21-foot, 4-inch aft measurement and a 22-foot forward measurement. This is from the halyard shackle to the transom. With the 11-inch bottom board, I use 21 feet, 6 inches aft and 22 feet, 2 inches forward.

The Bruder mast, which is no longer produced but is still on many Snipes, should have the same aft rake but less forward rake since it bends more than the Cobra.

Most Snipes are using 17-inch spreaders with swing limited only at the aft position and a tip to tip measurement there of 26 inches.

Mast step and jib tack should be as far forward as the class rules allow.

Shrouds / The Snipe allows considerable latitude in the chainplate location, and we're fairly well aft in the Eichenlaub and the Chubasco. With the Bruder mast, you can put your chainplates farther forward because of the tight rig, and this allows your boom to swing farther out downwind. On lakes, most sailors have their chainplates fairly well forward.

Jib Lead / Our lead is 15½ inches from centerline, and we don't use a barber hauler at all. I have a reaching hook that I use occasionally, and Jeff Lenhart didn't have either on his boat when he won the Pan American Games.

Centerboard / There are three types of boards legal in the Snipe class at this time: two with the straight front edge and one with the rounded front. The two straight boards differ in the width at the bottom of the board: either 6 inches or 11 inches. I prefer the 6-inch bottom for general racing, but the 11-inch board is the only one legal for the world's championship, and it will probably become the most often used. The 6-inch board changes the feel of the boat a bit and is harder to use; the round board is used quite a bit on lakes where the extra area helps them point higher.

Traveler / Snipe travelers are awkward becaue of the bridle. Most boats don't have the bridle with control lines on the sliding block, which means more difficulty in controlling the sail shape. You need to center the boom in light air, which is easy with the control lines, although they do clutter up the cockpit. Without the controls, you have to adjust the bridle length as far out as possible in light air and then strap it down in stronger winds.

Crew Placement / The crew should sit close together toward the front of the cockpit near the shroud. Downwind, sit on opposite sides of the boat and move aft when planing.

Boat Trim / Aside from heeling the boat to get the chine out of the water, the Snipe is pretty conventional. One small difference is that you don't have to heel to weather downwind as much, since it doesn't seem to add much speed.

Sail Trim / Because the only way you can keep the headstay tight is to sheet the main hard, you'll find that the Snipe is sheeted harder in all conditions than other boats. The jib is so far inboard at the lead that the Snipe just won't tolerate any sag in the luff, and most people don't sheet hard enough. You have to sail with almost no twist in the main at all.

Coronado – 15

Idiosyncrasies / The oddest thing about the C-15 is the fact that you have to sail with the traveler pulled all the way to weather at all times. Because the boom is so high, the mainsheet has a normal angle to it when the traveler is to weather.

Crew Size / The minimum is 300 pounds, and you should be as close to that as possible.

Mast Rake / We use a plumb bob from the main halyard shackle to check the angle of the mast. Our rig was a little bit loose and the mast was vertical in the forward position, and had a 9-inch rake (measured at the gooseneck level) when pulled aft. We used 17-inch spreaders stopped aft at 24 inches tip to tip, although some boats are now using fixed spreaders that are pre-loaded to keep the mast straight. The main problem with the C-15 is a very limber mast.

Centerboard / Should be set to use as much jibe as permitted by class rules.

Boat Trim / The only way to judge in a C-15 is to make sure that the knuckle of the bow is just barely into the water when going upwind. That keeps the boat level and it doesn't pound much. Keep the boat flat when trapezing, and let it heel slightly when the wind is light.

Figure 19 ■ *A crude but effective mast raker on a Coronado 15. A line leads up from the mast and through a bullet block, down to the base of the mast, and back to the helmsman. Pulling down the mast raker forces the mast aft, easing off on it allows the spar to bend.*

Sail Trim / The traveler has already been mentioned, but it relates to the mainsail trim since the C-15 needs more twist than will appear correct. If there isn't enough twist, the slot between main and jib will close up and the boat will slow down. So use the sheet and traveler to keep a considerable amount of mainsail twist.

Miscellaneous / The boat needs a mast partner badly, and I don't think you can be competitive without it. Blocks should be used to limit mast bend at the partners, or a block and tackle arrangement, now legal, will do the same thing.

Halyard locks would also be a good idea, especially since many boats are now using the floating luff jib which needs a very tight headstay.

Index